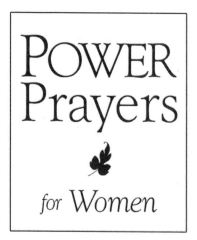

POWER
Prayers
for Women

JACKIE M. JOHNSON

BARBOUR
PUBLISHING

Published by Barbour Publishing, Inc., P.O. Box 719, Uhrichsville, Ohio 44683 www.barbourbooks.com

Our mission is to publish and distribute inspirational products offering exceptional value and biblical encouragement to the masses.

Member of the
Evangelical Christian
Publishers Association

Printed in the United States of America.

For my parents, Robert Johnson and Patti Ripani,
the ones who first taught me to pray.

Acknowledgments

Special thanks to Ken Gire for his encouragement and support, and to Judith Couchman for her advice, mentoring, and friendship. Thank you to my gracious and understanding editor at Barbour Publishing, Paul K. Muckley. I give my heartfelt gratitude to my family, friends, and Wednesday night Bible study group for your prayers that sustain me. You are loved and appreciated more than you know.

Contents

Introduction

The Power of Prayer

*There is not in the world a kind of life more sweet and delightful
than that of a continual conversation with God.*

<small>BROTHER LAWRENCE</small>

*L*ove, communication, and relationships are all important to women. We enjoy nurturing the bond of friendship by spending time together—whether we talk over coffee, scrapbook with friends, or volunteer together at a soup kitchen. We yearn to connect on a deep conversational level with our husbands or boyfriends. (Okay, we don't always get that, but we still yearn for it.) With our closest friends we share our longings and losses, desires and disappointments, struggles and secret dreams. Loving friendships bring us joy and fulfillment.

While emotional bonds with family and friends are essential to our well-being, so is our connection with God. That's really the most important relationship in life—and it can grow stronger and deeper as you get to know Him better. You can pursue friendship with God just as you would with another person—through conversation (prayer), learning more about the person (reading the Bible), and spending time with your friend (enjoying God's presence). From this wellspring of first love, everything else in life will flow.

Most of us want more loving relationships, more joy, more confidence, and more energy to live our best lives. We want our kids to be safe and to make wise decisions. We want more energy to balance the demands of work, ministry, family, and home. We want to be rid of our bad habits. We want to change—but we often lack the self-discipline or motivation to make change happen. That's why prayer is so important.

Prayer connects us to the One who has the power to make lasting change in our lives. It's a holy conversation, talking and listening to God Almighty, the One who loves us more than we will ever know. In fact, that's where the power in powerful prayers comes from: being connected.

Prayer Is a Love Connection with God

*H*ow is your love connection? Maybe you talk to God regularly, but you don't feel like you're getting through. Duty has replaced desire, and your quiet time feels dull, routine, or boring. Perhaps, like many people, you want to pray more consistently—but even though your intentions are good, you're too busy and distracted. You want results, but answers take longer than you think they should. And sometimes, when it seems like nothing is happening at all, you wonder if your prayers are working.

When that happens, it's time to get the "power" back in your prayers. How? By connecting and staying connected to the True Source, you could be positively transformed.

What Prayer Is — and Isn't

*P*rayer is multidimensional. Sometimes it's a calming oasis, a place of silence and solitude where you can find hope for a revitalized life. At other times it's a wrestling ring, where you struggle with God in a confessional, a chance to tell God what you've done wrong—and find forgiveness. In that freedom, prayer becomes a celebration as you thank God for all He's done for you and all He's yet to do. Finally, prayer can be a loveseat, an intimate place where the Lord whispers His love for you—and you say in return how much you adore Him. These blessings aren't limited to a particular devotional time—you can talk with God throughout the day in an ongoing conversation. Confessing, worshiping, and thanking God—simply enjoying His presence—are as much a part of prayer as asking for personal needs or interceding for others.

Prayer is not a magical set of words you use to get what you want. It's not based on how you feel. It's not judged by how long you pray, or how loud, or if you use the right words. When you pray in faith, simply and sincerely, each prayer is a powerful moment in God's Spirit.

Getting Connected

*P*ower prayers start with getting connected. Suppose, for example, you want to play your favorite music on the radio. You'd plug the radio's cord into an electrical socket. With that connection, electricity provides the power you need. But what if you tried inserting the plug into the carpet? Nothing. It simply wouldn't work, because carpet is not an energy source.

Many of us try to "plug in" to alternative power sources in our lives, things like money, prestige, the praise of others—even caffeine and chocolate. But none of those are connections that bring life. Only one Source can do that. For the real thing, the true source of power, we connect to God. And we maintain that connection through prayer, allowing His Holy Spirit to empower and energize our lives.

Staying Connected

*T*hough it may seem hard to believe, a truly different—more powerful—prayer life is within your reach. *Power Prayers for Women* will help you get started. Each chapter contains a brief overview of an important prayer focus—from your marriage, children, friends, and extended family, to your finances, fears, ministry, and life goals. At the end of each chapter, you'll find specific prayers on various topics, to be read complete or as "starter prayers"—outlines to which you add your own words as you continue praying. Most important, each of the prayers is derived from scripture, so you'll be "praying the Word," the most powerful way to pray!

Praying God's Word Is Powerful

*I*n *Power Prayers for Women,* you'll discover the power of God's Word, the power of forgiveness, the power of worship, and the power of faith. Every chapter will introduce you to a different aspect of God's power—and you'll be encouraged and strengthened.

Powerful prayer is about connecting to God, growing in Him, and being transformed. Are you ready to energize your prayers? Let's get started, and light up the rest of your life!

Lord, I long to be more connected to You. Teach me to worship You as the true source of power and love. I adore You like no other. Teach me to pray. Change me, Lord. Transform me so my prayers will be powerful and my life will be fruitful. And may all that I do bring glory to Your name. In Jesus' name, amen.

The Power of God's Word

For everything that was written in the past was written to teach us,
so that through endurance and the encouragement
of the Scriptures we might have hope.

ROMANS 15:4

*A*dventure, danger, romance—just a few story themes from the best-selling book of all time. Undoubtedly, billions of copies have been printed and distributed.

Unlike fairy tales, this book is true and starts with, "In the beginning." Here you learn of kings and conquerors, love and loss, rebellion and redemption. Turn the pages to discover where you came from, why you are here, and where you are going. You'll find out how to handle money and have better relationships. Most important, you can learn who God is and how you can live with Him forever.

What is this astonishing book? The Bible. Inspired by God, this sixty-six-book compilation is the true story of God's love for all people, including you and me. It's the explanation of a promised deliverance, and freedom for all who obey.

"All Scripture," according to 2 Timothy 3:16–17, "is God-breathed and is useful for teaching, rebuking, correcting and training in righteousness, so that the man of God may be thoroughly equipped for every good work." The Bible is the believer's instruction manual for living.

The Bible is sacred and revered—because it is life-giving and powerful. Despite the opposition of modern culture, God's Word stands strong, providing truth in an age of relativism, light in the darkness of deception or depression, and cool refreshment for the challenge of everyday living. Scripture provides encouragement, convicts us of wrongdoing, and teaches us how to live in forgiveness, love, and victory.

The power of God's Word is available to you every day. Do you need to break a bad habit or addiction? Do you need to change your attitude or love your husband or have more patience with your kids? Perhaps you seek a new perspective or healing for your physical body or broken heart. Could you use more joy and less stress in your life? The Bible offers healing and comfort, truth and perspective, and the power to transform lives. In other words, it provides the power to live each day and have hope for the future.

Power for supernatural living comes as we ingest God's Word, feeding on it as we would a delicious meal. Let it nourish you as spiritual food. Reflect on it, meditate on it, speak and pray it aloud in your quiet times with the Lord. Commit key verses to memory so you will have them when you need comfort or strength. Finally, take action. *Live* the words you've read. Jesus said, "If you love me, you will obey what I command" (John 14:15).

Like a stone dropped into a pond, the ripple effect of a loving, obedient response to God's Word can go far beyond what you may ever know—your own life, your family, your community, your nation, and your world.

God's Word Is Truth

To the Jews who had believed him, Jesus said, "If you hold to my teaching, you are really my disciples. Then you will know the truth, and the truth will set you free."

*T*hank You, Lord, that Your Word is true. Sometimes it's hard to discern truth from a lie, or from the half-truths that bombard me daily from the television, radio, magazines, and popular culture. I want to know the truth and live it. Help me to look to Your steady and solid Word, not to this world, for my life instruction manual. I thank You that You will never lead me astray, that You never lie to me, and that You always keep Your promises.

Light for Understanding

Your word is a lamp to my feet and a light for my path.

PSALM 119:105

*L*ord, Your Word is a lamp in my darkness—a flashlight on the path of life that helps me see the way. Your words enlighten me with wisdom, insight, and hope, even when I cannot see where I am going or how things will turn out. I'm so glad that You know the right direction. You have gone before me and are always with me, so I don't need to be afraid. I choose to follow Your leading.

Spiritual Refreshment

*Listen, O heavens, and I will speak; hear, O earth, the words of my mouth.
Let my teaching fall like rain and my words descend like dew, like showers
on new grass, like abundant rain on tender plants. I will proclaim the
name of the LORD. Oh, praise the greatness of our God!*

DEUTERONOMY 32:1–3

*L*ord, I thank You for Your words that speak to my heart and
needs. I long to soak in Your teaching and learn more about
You. Your life-giving messages are like rain showers on new,
green grass. I need not just a sprinkle, but a downpour—a
soaking, abundant rain in my dry heart! Even though life
can be challenging, I will proclaim the name of the Lord and
praise the greatness of our God!

Life-Giving Bread

*Jesus answered, "It is written: 'Man does not live on bread alone,
but on every word that comes from the mouth of God.'"*

MATTHEW 4:4

*Y*our Word is my daily nourishment, Lord. Thank You
for the Bread of Life You provide every single day. Those
words feed and nurture my soul just as eating bread fills
me and provides the nutrition I need to live. Without Your
words I will fade and die spiritually; with them I am vibrant,
energized, and alive! Be my portion, Lord, as I seek You.
And not just Your hands and what You give, but also Your
face, Lord. I desire to know who You really are.

Steady Hope

I wait for the LORD, my soul waits,
and in his word I put my hope.
PSALM 130:5

*L*ord, so many times I am tempted to think that people or things will satisfy me. But often they leave me empty and unfulfilled. Help me to remember that You are the source of my hope—not a man, or a better job, or a pan of brownies. Those are all good things, but they will never fully satisfy me like You do. Forgive me for misplaced hope. Help me to put my trust in You and Your secure, steady, and unfailing love.

God's Word Is Powerful

*For the word of God is living and active. Sharper than any double-edged
sword, it penetrates even to dividing soul and spirit, joints and marrow;
it judges the thoughts and attitudes of the heart.*

HEBREWS 4:12

*T*hank You for Your life-changing words that reveal the
true condition of my heart. I can't hide it from You, for You
already know everything. But with Your conviction comes
repentance and forgiveness. You accept me as I am and give
me the grace and power to make real and lasting changes in
my life. The Word of God is living and active. That's why
it has so much power. I give You my thoughts and attitudes
and ask for healing.

Equipped for Good Work

*All Scripture is God-breathed and is useful for teaching, rebuking,
correcting and training in righteousness, so that the man of God
may be thoroughly equipped for every good work.*

2 TIMOTHY 3:16–17

*L*ord, I want to be equipped to live this life as a Christ-
follower. You breathed Your life into the words that men
put on parchment—which are now the words of the Bible I
read. Teach me, Lord. Help me to accept Your rebuke when
I need it. Correct and train me in righteousness so that I will
be ready for whatever life holds for me today.

The Way to Eternal Life

*From infancy you have known the holy Scriptures, which
are able to make you wise for salvation through faith in Christ Jesus.*

2 TIMOTHY 3:15

*L*ord, I thank You for signposts You provide in Your
Word—for Your directions to heaven. The Bible helps me to
be "wise for salvation through faith in Christ Jesus." What a
privilege it is to know You through reading about Your Son.
He reveals to me what love really is and accepts me just the
way I am. You are the Way, the Truth, and the Life, and I
choose to follow You.

Wisdom in Interpretation

*Do your best to present yourself to God as one approved,
a workman who does not need to be ashamed
and who correctly handles the word of truth.*

2 TIMOTHY 2:15

*L*ord, I am Your student. Teach me to read Your Word,
meditate on it, and apply it to my life. Give me a hunger for
spending time with You—and wisdom when I teach Your
Word to others. I want to be a person who correctly handles
the Word of Truth. I ask the Holy Spirit to enlighten me and
give me understanding that I may live right and bring glory
to Your name.

Revive Me!

*The law of the LORD is perfect, reviving the soul. The statutes of the
LORD are trustworthy, making wise the simple.*

PSALM 19:7

*L*ord, sometimes life gets so crazy. I get so tired and stressed
out from working hard at my job—whether it's in the home
or in the marketplace. I long to bask in Your presence and
find refreshment. Revive my soul with Your Word. Immerse
my life in Your life-giving truth, turning the dark places to
light so I can radiate Jesus in my corner of the world.

Give Me Joy

*The precepts of the LORD are right, giving joy to the heart.
The commands of the LORD are radiant, giving light to the eyes.*

PSALM 19:8

*L*ord, Your words are right and true; they bring joy to my
heart. I need more joy in my life. Happiness comes and goes,
but joy is deep and lasting. This world can take so much out
of me with the cares of the day, pressures from my job, and
commitments I've made. I need Your true joy despite my
circumstances and my feelings. Your commands illuminate
me so I can sing Your praises and live revitalized each day.
Thank You for Your joy, Lord.

To Know God's Will

*For this reason, since the day we heard about you,
we have not stopped praying for you and asking
God to fill you with the knowledge of his will through
all spiritual wisdom and understanding.*
COLOSSIANS 1:9

Lord, I want to know Your will for my life. Enlighten me with wisdom, discernment, and understanding. I need to know when to stay and when to go, when to speak and when to close my mouth. Fill me with the knowledge of Your best for me—right now and in the future. As I seek to follow You, help me to obediently and joyfully accept Your answers.

Be Doers of the Word

Do not merely listen to the word, and so deceive yourselves. Do what it says.
Anyone who listens to the word but does not do what it says is like a man who
looks at his face in a mirror and, after looking at himself, goes away and immediately
forgets what he looks like. But the man who looks intently into the perfect law
that gives freedom, and continues to do this, not forgetting what he has heard,
but doing it—he will be blessed in what he does.

JAMES 1:22–25

*L*ord, I want to be a woman of action. I don't just want to hear or read the Bible; I want to do what it says. I want to live what I believe! Help me not to be deceived or forget what my eyes have just read. I look to the Bible for truth and freedom so I can live, with love and victory, the abundant life you promise to all who believe. I look to Your Word and ask for Your blessings.

Memorize the Word

I have hidden your word in my heart
that I might not sin against you.

PSALM 119:11

*L*ord, I thank You for Your words that bring life and healing. They comfort me and give me strength when I need it. I want to hide the Word in my heart that I might not sin against You, that I may live in abundance and favor and seek to know You better. Help me to memorize Your scripture so it's on my tongue and in my heart when I need it. May I always be ready to speak the truth in love.

My Salvation

The Power of Grace and Forgiveness

*"For God did not send his Son into the world to condemn the world,
but to save the world through him."*

JOHN 3:17

*M*y grandfather was a carpenter. He built the first house I lived in as a child. I was only four years old, but I still remember when workers laid the gray blocks of the foundation, raised the wooden beams, finished the roof, and completed the landscaping. I was fascinated with the building process, as an empty field was being transformed into a place I would soon call "home."

I have always been interested in origins. Knowing how things begin provides insight and perspective, a framework of reference. The source of the power in "power prayers" is a connection with the origin of life and power—it is a connection with God through a relationship with His Son, Jesus Christ. Thankfully, anyone can find that connection. It all starts with a simple prayer.

Many people know *about* God, but they don't always take the time to know Him personally. They are, as author Max Lucado says, "close to the Cross—but far from Christ."[1] Some mistakenly think they can earn their way to heaven through good works, money, or performance. But, no matter how hard you try, you can't make it to heaven on your own merit. Salvation is the *gift* of God, one that each person needs to receive for herself. As Ephesians 2:8–9 says, "For it is by grace you have been saved, through faith—and this not from yourselves, it is the gift of God—not by works, so that no one can boast."

Ultimately, each of us needs to decide about God. In *The Case for Faith*, former atheist Lee Strobel asked himself, "Did I *want* to know God personally—to experience release from guilt, to live the way I was designed to live, to pursue his purposes for my life, to tap into his power for daily living, to commune with him in this life and for eternity in the next? If so, there was plenty of evidence upon which to base a rational decision to say 'yes' to him. It was up to me—just as it's up to you." [2]

When you know Jesus in this deeper way, you learn the startling power of unconditional love and acceptance, a knowledge that leads to transformation. I've experienced it personally, and I have seen it in others. Forgiveness, transformation, and changed lives are the fruit of redemption.

Romans 10:9 states, "If you confess with your mouth, 'Jesus is Lord,' and believe in your heart that God raised him from the dead, you will be saved." If you have never prayed to receive Christ into your life, why not do so now? In the prayer section following, there's a helpful prayer you can use. If you are already a Christ-follower, take time to thank God for the gift of your salvation.

Praying to receive Jesus into your life is the prerequisite to powerful Christian living. Connected to the power of God, your prayer life—and your entire life—will be ignited and energized.

Prayer for Salvation

If you confess with your mouth, "Jesus is Lord," and believe in your heart that God raised him from the dead, you will be saved.

ROMANS 10:9

*L*ord, I humbly bow before you now and confess my sins to you. I am sorry for all of my wrongdoing, and I ask Your forgiveness. I believe Jesus is the Son of God, and that He died on a cross and was raised from the dead. He conquered death so that I might really live—in power and purpose here on earth and forever with Him in heaven. I choose You. Please be my Savior and my Lord.

Thank You for Saving Me

Thanks be to God for his indescribable gift!

2 CORINTHIANS 9:15

*L*ord, I thank you for my salvation. I thank you for Your indescribable gift of eternal life and the power to do Your will today. I can hardly fathom how you suffered, yet You did it all for me—for every person on this planet. Mocked and beaten, You bled for my sins. You had victory over death so I could live. You made a way for me, and I am eternally grateful. Thank you, Lord.

A New Beginning

Therefore, if anyone is in Christ, he is a new creation;
the old has gone, the new has come!

2 CORINTHIANS 5:17

*L*ord, now that I am devoted to You heart and soul, I am a new creation. Thank You for washing away my old ways of thinking and behaving, and for empowering me to live a new life. Your love changes me! Help me to live this new life with wisdom, making the right choices. Give me the courage to love the way You love. Teach me Your ways as we journey together on this path toward heaven. . .toward home.

Grace Alone

For it is by grace you have been saved, through faith—
and this not from yourselves, it is the gift of God—
not by works, so that no one can boast.

EPHESIANS 2:8–9

*L*ord, You give the best gifts! I receive the love gift of my salvation, knowing that it is by grace that I have been saved, through faith. I didn't do anything to deserve it or earn it. I know my works did not save me, for if they did, then I could boast about it. Instead, You saved me by grace so I can now do good works—things you prepared in advance for me to do—to bring glory to Your name.

Only Jesus Saves

*"Salvation is found in no one else, for there is
no other name under heaven given to
men by which we must be saved."*
ACTS 4:12

*L*ord, Your Word says that salvation is found in no one else but God's Son, Jesus Christ. Only His name has the power to save. Our society likes to propose alternative ideas and try to convince me that I can find life in other ways—buying more things or finding romance or looking a certain way. Not true! I choose to believe in Jesus, not in other gods, not in other religious philosophies, not in materialism. Thank you for Your power to save.

Energized Living

By his power God raised the Lord from
the dead, and he will raise us also.
1 CORINTHIANS 6:14

*L*ord, I am truly amazed at Your great power. By the power of God, Jesus was raised from the dead. And You will raise me, too. You lift my spirits from sadness to joy. You give me energy when my kids have depleted me. You help me find funds when my car needs repair. You give me friends to encourage me and share my life with. You heal bodies and broken relationships. Thank You for the power to live this life every day.

Forgiven

"All the prophets testify about him that everyone who
believes in him receives forgiveness of sins through his name."
ACTS 10:43

*L*ord, I am grateful for Your forgiveness. It's Your name, the name of Jesus, that covers our sins when we believe in You. As I receive Your pardon, empower me to have mercy on others. I thank You that I am forgiven and free. Please help me to forgive others when they've hurt me, knowing that You are the One who brings justice. And please give me the power to forgive myself, too.

Restored Relationships

Know that a man is not justified by observing the law, but
by faith in Jesus Christ. So we, too, have put our faith in
Christ Jesus that we may be justified by faith in Christ and not by
observing the law, because by observing the law no one will be justified.

GALATIANS 2:16

*L*ord, You know how painful it is when things are not right between friends. I long for connected relationships, where people live in peace and harmony and there is no resentment between them. What a joy it is to know that I am made right with God by faith. We can communicate freely, talking and listening, enjoying each other as heart friends. I want to live in a growing love relationship with You. Thank You for restoration and righteousness.

God's Presence

"The virgin will be with child and will give birth to a son,
and they will call him Immanuel"—which means, "God with us."

MATTHEW 1:23

*L*ord, I thank You for sending Your Son, God with Us, Emmanuel. Born of a virgin, You came to point us to the truth that saves us. You chose twelve disciples who followed You and learned the way to really live. You healed the sick; You gave sight to the blind. You were known for Your miracles and Your radical love for all kinds of people. Thank You for Your presence and for living in me today.

To Love and Obey

*Jesus replied, "If anyone loves me, he will obey my teaching. My Father
will love him, and we will come to him and make our home with him."*

JOHN 14:23

*L*ord, I love You. And because of that I choose to obey You. Teach me Your ways as You make Your home in me. Clean out my cupboards of selfishness, and wash away the negative thoughts from my closets. Change my wrong ways of thinking—about myself and others—so I can be a vessel of hope and light. Help me to know You better. . .to be a doer of the word, not just a hearer. . .to live what I believe.

Not Ashamed

*I am not ashamed of the gospel, because it is the power
of God for the salvation of everyone who believes: first
for the Jew, then for the Gentile.*

ROMANS 1:16

*L*ord, I am not ashamed of the gospel. Your words have the power to bring salvation to every person who believes. I don't want to hide the light of truth, but instead to let it shine from my life so others will see Christ in me. When people ask me about the source of my joy, give me the words to share so they can know You, too. Help me bring glory to You as I stand with courage and strength in the truth.

Let's Grow

Like newborn babies, crave pure spiritual milk,
so that by it you may grow up in your salvation.
1 PETER 2:2

*L*ord, I want to grow up spiritually. I want to transition from a newborn baby who drinks only milk to a more mature believer who craves the "meat" of deeper things. I want to move from head knowledge to heart experience with You. I want to know what it means to enjoy Your presence, not just to make requests. Step by step and day by day, teach me to follow and learn Your ways.

I Will Follow You

*Then he said to them all: "If anyone would come after me, he must
deny himself and take up his cross daily and follow me. For whoever
wants to save his life will lose it, but whoever loses his life for me will save it."*
LUKE 9:23–24

*L*ord, here I am before You. I am ready to "take up my cross"
and follow You. Every day I want to be with You, empowered
by You, and loved so deeply that I am changed. Show me
what it means to lose my life in order to save it. Teach me
about surrender, knowing You lift me up to do Your good
purposes. Transform me, Lord. Teach me to follow You.

Words of Life

*Simon Peter answered him, "Lord, to whom shall we go?
You have the words of eternal life."*
JOHN 6:68

*L*ord, you have the words of eternal life that allow us to
cross over from death to life, from bondage to freedom, and
from misery to peace. Words can be so hurtful at times, but
Your words bring life, hope, and healing. You did not come
to condemn me, but to save me and free me from death. Fill
me with Your words of life and hope so I may use them to
encourage others.

The Power of a Renewed Mind

Be transformed by the renewing of your mind.
ROMANS 12:2

*L*indy has a successful career in financial services. After her sixty-hour work weeks, she rarely has the energy to initiate friendships. Instead, Lindy arrives home late, pops a frozen dinner into the microwave, flips on the television, and sinks into the couch until bedtime. While she is pleasant and competent at the office, Lindy is lonely and isolated in the rest of her life.

Erin is angry, though she doesn't want anyone to know that. Her two teenage daughters—once her sweet, carefree little girls—are disobedient and disrespectful. They like to party every night, even during the school week, and Erin feels helpless to stop them. She wants her friends to think she's a capable mother, so she hides her emotions with a continual smile. Like a duck gliding across the water, she appears calm on the surface—but in reality, she's paddling wildly just to stay afloat. Erin wants to scream, "Doesn't anyone know how much pain I'm in?" But instead she replies with a cheery, "Oh, I'm fine!" when anyone asks how she's doing.

Emotions are a normal part of life. As human beings, each of us has a full range of emotions—love, happiness, joy, delight, peace, disappointment, loss, grief, doubt, compassion, sadness, depression, jealousy, anger, bitterness, guilt, and many others. We are happy when a friend comes to visit, we are sad when our dog dies, and we are frustrated when we can't seem to lose weight.

Throughout the Bible, women and men—even Jesus—display a variety of emotions. I imagine that Adam and Eve were deliriously happy in the Garden of Eden. The woman caught in adultery and pushed before a condemning crowd must have felt humiliation. Mary, the virgin mother of Jesus, was fearful when she learned she was pregnant, then joyful when she discovered the news was true—she would give birth to the Savior of the world! David was afraid for his life while Saul pursued him with murderous intent. And Jesus felt alone, broken to the point of sweating blood, as He prayed for His life to be spared.

Emotions, whether positive or negative, can be powerful—even overwhelming at times. Managing those emotions is a part of maturity. When our emotions aren't processed in healthy ways, they can get stuck like a clogged drain. Help comes when we surrender our feelings to the One who has the power to blast away our emotional congestion.

Prayer is essential to managing emotions. In fact, it transforms us. Praying powerfully for this area of our lives can begin with praying 2 Corinthians 10:5, asking God to help us "take captive every thought to make it obedient to Christ." To change how we feel, we need to adjust the way we think. When we alter the way we view our situations, we can change the way we respond to them—with wisdom, rather than impulsive actions we may regret later.

With God's help, we can get through both the valleys and the victories of life.

God and Emotions

"The LORD is slow to anger, abounding in
love and forgiving sin and rebellion."
NUMBERS 14:18

*L*ord, what a blessing You are that You have given us such an array of emotions with which to express ourselves. Help me to be more like You—slow to anger and abounding in love. Help me to be a woman who is forgiving. I pray for more discernment, so that in whatever comes my way I will have the grace to think, speak, and act with a good and godly attitude.

Renewing Your Mind

Do not conform any longer to the pattern of this world, but be transformed
by the renewing of your mind. Then you will be able to test
and approve what God's will is—his good, pleasing and perfect will.
ROMANS 12:2

*L*ord, sometimes I feel like my emotions need a makeover. Renovate me—transform me so I can be balanced and healthy in my emotions. I ask for your power to change. I don't want to be the way I used to be. I want to be wise and enjoy sound thinking. I want to make good decisions in how I express myself in my words and actions. Help me to know Your will and have a mind that's renewed.

Joy

Our mouths were filled with laughter,
our tongues with songs of joy.
PSALM 126:2

*L*ord, thank You for the gift of laughter! I thank You for the joy You bring into my life through a child's smile, a luscious peach, a hot bath, and a good night's sleep. Help me remember that when I am "looking up" to You, Lord, I can have a more optimistic outlook and be a more positive person. Keep my eyes on You, not myself or my circumstances, so I can live with a lighter, more joy-filled heart.

Confidence

Have no fear of sudden disaster or of the ruin that overtakes
the wicked, for the LORD will be your confidence and
will keep your foot from being snared.
PROVERBS 3:25–26

*L*ord, I want to be a more confident woman. I don't want to be afraid of disasters—or just making mistakes. Give me the courage to know that You, Lord, will be my confidence. You keep me from tripping over my tongue and saying the wrong thing. But even when I do, You have the power to make things right again. Thank You for the confidence You give me. Let me walk with my head high because I know who I am in Christ: I am Yours!

Compassion

*Be kind and compassionate to one another, forgiving
each other, just as in Christ God forgave you.*
EPHESIANS 4:32

*L*ord, Your compassion for people is great. You healed the blind and You led the people who were lost like sheep without a shepherd. Create in me a heart of compassion—enlarge my vision so I see and help the poor, the sick, the people who don't know You, and the people whose concerns You lay upon my heart. Help me never to be so busy or self-absorbed that I overlook my family and friends who may need my assistance.

Needing Encouragement

*May our Lord Jesus Christ himself and God our Father, who loved us
and by his grace gave us eternal encouragement and good hope,
encourage your hearts and strengthen you in every good deed and word.*
2 THESSALONIANS 2:16–17

*L*ord, I need encouragement. Will You please inspire my heart and strengthen me in everything I say and do? I need Your truth to lift my spirit and help me soar. Let me be like an eagle that glides on the wind. Give me the courage and energy I need to keep going even when I'm weary.

Stress

*Cast your cares on the LORD and he will sustain you;
he will never let the righteous fall.*
PSALM 55:22

*L*ord, I can't take one more day of this hectic whirl of life—the traffic, the crying kids, my workload at the office, and everything else I have to handle. Sometimes it just feels like too much! Help me to breathe out my cares, casting them away like line from a fishing rod. But don't let me reel them back in! Here is my burned out, anxious heart. May Your oceans of love and power replenish me, providing the energy I need to do what You want me to do each day.

Loneliness

"Surely I am with you always, to the very end of the age."
MATTHEW 28:20

*L*ord, I thank You that You are my true companion—that I am never alone. You have assigned angels to watch over and protect me. You have given me Your Holy Spirit and promised that You are with me always, even to the very end of the age. What a privilege that You call me Your friend. As we travel this road of life together, on city sidewalks, suburban roads, or country paths, I enjoy Your presence, Lord. Help me never to forget Your presence.

Anger

Get rid of all bitterness, rage and anger, brawling and slander, along with every form of malice.
EPHESIANS 4:31

*L*ord, I am so mad! I am angry, and I need Your help. Why do things have to go so wrong? I need to do something with this heated emotion—and I choose to give You my anger and bitterness, Lord. Help me be rid of it. Redeem the confusion and bring peace to what seems so out of control. Free me from resentment and blame. Show me my part in this conflict as You speak to the heart of my adversary. I need your healing and peace, Lord.

Healing Guilt and Shame

For day and night your hand was heavy upon me; my strength was sapped as in the heat of summer. Selah. Then I acknowledged my sin to you and did not cover up my iniquity. I said, "I will confess my transgressions to the LORD"—and you forgave the guilt of my sin. Selah. Therefore let everyone who is godly pray to you while you may be found; surely when the mighty waters rise, they will not reach him.

PSALM 32:4–6

*L*ord, my shame makes me want to hide. But I can no longer hide in the darkness of my guilt and sin. You already know everything I've done wrong, yet You bring me into the light—not to condemn, nor to condone, but to heal me. I acknowledge my wrongs and confess them all to You, Lord. I stand in Your forgiveness as the cleansing water of Your gentle love flows over me, washing away my guilt and shame.

Sadness

Why are you downcast, O my soul? Why so disturbed within me? Put your hope in God, for I will yet praise him.

PSALM 42:5

*L*ord, I feel so gloomy today. Do you see my tears? In my sadness, help me to remember that even when I'm down, I can choose to put my hope in You. Instead of telling myself lies that push me deeper into despair, I can look to Your truth. Remind me of the good things You have done in the past. I choose to praise You. You are my Savior and my God. May Your love comfort me now.

Depression

He lifted me out of the slimy pit, out of the mud and mire; he set my feet on a rock and gave me a firm place to stand. He put a new song in my mouth, a hymn of praise to our God. Many will see and fear and put their trust in the LORD.
PSALM 40:2–3

*L*ord, will you please change the music of my life from a sad, minor key to a joy-filled, major key? Give me a new song to sing, a happier tune! It's amazing to me that there is no mess too big for You to fix, no broken life too shattered for You to restore, and no loss too great for You to redeem. As You raise me out of the darkness of my slimy pit, lifting me from the mud and mire of my depression to solid emotional ground, I will praise You.

Hope for Confusion

"But now, Lord, what do I look for? My hope is in you."
PSALM 39:7

*L*ord, I am so confused! I don't know what to do—and I need Your wisdom. I know that You are a God who delights in clarity and order, not chaos and confusion. Lead me on the right course of action; show me when to speak and when to be silent, when to move and when to be still. I don't know what to do, but You certainly do. As I wait on You for guidance, help me to listen and follow Your ways.

Foolish Disobedience

At one time we too were foolish, disobedient, deceived and enslaved by all kinds of passions and pleasures. We lived in malice and envy, being hated and hating one another. But when the kindness and love of God our Savior appeared, he saved us, not because of righteous things we had done, but because of his mercy. He saved us through the washing of rebirth and renewal by the Holy Spirit.

TITUS 3:3–5

*L*ord, I have done many foolish things—and I am sorry. I don't want to be disobedient. I have made unwise choices, and I have been deceived and taken captive by the passions and pleasures of the world. Forgive me. Thank You for saving me by Your mercy and a love that's hard to fathom. Sometimes Your kindness startles me—in spite of all I have done wrong, You bring me back to Your good graces. Thank You, gracious Lord.

The Power of Love

My lover is mine and I am his.
SONG OF SONGS 2:16

*L*ove is like a fire: It needs to be tended in order to burn brightly. In a similar way, good marriages don't just happen—they need attention. If left alone, both a fire and a marriage will eventually burn out, leaving only a pile of ashes in place of a warm glow.

Marriage is the deepest connection we can have with another human being—and it was God's good idea. "For this reason a man will leave his father and mother and be united to his wife, and they will become one flesh" (Genesis 2:24). With the person we love most in the world, we share companionship and intimacy. But sometimes "the ties that bind" can unravel—and we need to restore the connection.

The emotional ties in the lives of Karen and Don had been severely severed. After twenty-six years of marriage, the couple had come to a place where they "hated" each other—and wanted to give up. Then Karen attended a meeting at church called Prayer Shield for Families and learned she could serve her husband by praying for him.

Although she didn't feel like it, Karen began to pray for Don—and other women in the group prayed with her. Instead of focusing on his weaknesses, Karen prayed blessings and promises from God's Word over Don. She chose to demonstrate in her actions that she loved him in spite of it all.

Hard as that was, Karen remained soft before God, never shutting up her heart in bitterness or resentment. As she obediently persevered in prayer, love for Don was released into her heart. Today Karen and Don are walking strong again as a husband and wife who love and care for each other. Prayer changed him and humbled her heart, too.

The power of God's unconditional, never-ending, healing love can restore the hardest of hearts. "We fight the enemy's weapons of hatred and indifference with the Lord's weapon of love," says author Claire Cloninger.[3]

Today more than ever, we need to pray for healthy, intact marriages. Satan works overtime through our upside-down society, seeking to tear apart loyal marriages and loving families. The surest way to keep our homes' "state of the union" strong is to be intentional about harnessing the power of love—by reconnecting to God through the power of prayer.

Many Christian couples do not realize the value of praying together. That can draw us closer to God and to each other and can release power into our lives and marriages. Jesus said, "Again, I tell you that if two of you on earth agree about anything you ask for, it will be done for you by my Father in heaven. For where two or three come together in my name, there am I with them" (Matthew 18:19–20).

When God is honored first, marriage will be joyful and fulfilling.

Lord, Change Me

Search me, O God, and know my heart; test me and know my anxious thoughts. See
if there is any offensive way in me, and lead me in the way everlasting.

PSALM 139:23–24

*L*ord, look into my life and search my heart. Is there anything hurtful that I have been doing? Remove the sin and selfishness. Help me to stop focusing on how my husband should change. Lord, cleanse *my* heart first. I can't change anyone else, so I ask You to show me what needs to go from my life, what needs to stay, and how I can be right with You. As You do, I pray for greater love and healing in our marriage.

Love Each Other

Above all, love each other deeply, because
love covers over a multitude of sins.

1 PETER 4:8

*L*ord, You are the author of love. Teach us to love each other deeply, from the heart. I thank You for the love my husband and I share, for the joy and the closeness. When we do something wrong, help each of us to forgive and move past the offense. I pray that our love would be patient and kind, not proud or selfish, but seeking each other's good. Protect our love and keep our marriage solid as we put our hope and trust in You.

Respect Each Other

Wives, submit to your husbands, as is fitting in the Lord.
COLOSSIANS 3:18

*L*ord, I ask that my husband and I would value each other. As he loves me, help me to respect him. As I value him, help him to cherish me. Teach us to give and to receive in the ways that are meaningful to each of us. Help us both to be better listeners and to seek to understand. Lord, draw us always closer to You and to each other.

A Wife of Noble Character

A wife of noble character who can find?
She is worth far more than rubies.
PROVERBS 31:10

*L*ord, help me to be a wife of noble character. Reveal to me the worth and value that You have placed on me so that I don't try to follow what the world says. I want to be valuable to my husband, like a precious gem. I pray he will have full confidence in me as I seek to bring him good, not harm, all the days of my life. Clothe me with strength and dignity. Help me to be faithful, to handle life with a positive attitude, and to speak with wisdom.

Deal with Anger

"In your anger do not sin": Do not let the sun
go down while you are still angry.
EPHESIANS 4:26

*L*ord, I need Your help in dealing with my anger, whether I am simply annoyed, a little mad, or downright furious. I want to handle this feeling in healthy ways. Help me to process my emotions and not let them fester inside me. Help me to control my temper and talk about what bothers me in calmer ways. Show me how to give my anger to You so I can live in peace with my husband.

Forgive Each Other

Get rid of all bitterness, rage and anger, brawling
and slander, along with every form of malice.
EPHESIANS 4:31

*L*ord, I don't know why forgiveness can sometimes be so hard. We need Your help to get rid of bitterness and anger in our marriage. Help us to build each other up instead of putting each other down—even when it seems we deserve the latter. Teach us grace. Help us to forgive one another and to be kind and compassionate, because we know Christ forgave each of us.

Live in Unity

Be completely humble and gentle; be patient, bearing with one another in love. Make
every effort to keep the unity of the Spirit through the bond of peace.
EPHESIANS 4:2–3

*L*ord, I humbly ask that we would be united and strong as a couple. May Your cords of peace, honor, respect, and love hold us together during both the good times and the challenges of our married life. As we become more connected to You, Lord, help us to be closer to each other. Help us to be patient, bearing with one another in love. And help us to live in joyful harmony.

Live in Peace

A quarrelsome wife is like a constant dripping.
PROVERBS 19:13

*L*ord, sometime our house is anything but still—yet I want to live in peace. May I have serenity in my heart even when all else is constant motion. Help me to be a peacemaker, not a quarrelsome wife. I don't want to be like a constantly dripping faucet, an annoyance to him—I want to be a blessing. Help me give up my need for control. Empower me to accept my husband, respect him, and be a person of peace.

Better Communication

*Instead, speaking the truth in love, we will in all
things grow up into him who is the Head, that is, Christ.*
EPHESIANS 4:15

*L*ord, I thank You for my wonderful husband. I truly love him, but I need more; I need better communication with him. Help me not to fear asking for what I need emotionally. I pray that You would speak to his heart, and that he would learn to listen. Help him to ask me questions about my life and to be present in the conversation. Lord, help us to speak the truth in love and grow closer through better communication.

Revive Us, Lord

He who refreshes others will himself be refreshed.
PROVERBS 11:25

*L*ord, we need a revival in our marriage. I ask that you would restore the connection in our emotions and intimacy. Daily living tires us, and we need time together for true closeness, not just familiarity. I pray that we can rediscover the joy of our love for each other. I want to hold hands and hearts again. Unhurry us, Lord, so we can notice each other and nurture our marriage.

Reignite the Romance

Let him kiss me with the kisses of his mouth —
for your love is more delightful than wine.
SONG OF SONGS 1:2

*L*ord, I ask that You would reignite the romance, the chemistry, in my relationship with my husband. The fire of love sometimes dims—and we need it to burn brightly again. Fuel our intimacy with restored affection and passion for each other. Help us to remember the days when we were so eager: I am his! He is mine! And though our relationship has matured, help us always to find fulfillment in this God-ordained expression of love for one another.

Keep Us from Wandering

Marriage should be honored by all, and the marriage bed kept
pure, for God will judge the adulterer and all the sexually immoral.
HEBREWS 13:4

*L*ord, I ask in the name and power of Jesus that You would keep my husband and me from straying from our marriage vows. Keep our eyes from wandering and our hearts pure— toward you and toward each other—so that we never give in to emotional or sexual intimacy outside our marriage. Help us not to discredit our union but rather to stay faithful—and to cherish the special connecting bond we have with each other.

Fun and Friendship

He who finds a wife finds what is good
and receives favor from the LORD.
PROVERBS 18:22

*L*ord, I thank You for the bond of friendship in our marriage. I enjoy talking and sharing life with my husband. Thank You for our laughter and joy. Help us to keep our attitude positive, to smile and have fun together. Give us time to reconnect on a playful level—in sports, games, travel, or working together around the house. Keep us connected in love and friendship, and help us to truly enjoy each other.

For My Husband's Salvation

"God so loved the world that he gave his one and only Son,
that whoever believes in him shall not perish but have eternal life."
JOHN 3:16

*L*ord, I pray for my husband, asking that he would have a desire to know You. You would like everyone to find eternal life—and I pray for the One I love to know and experience Your love. I pray that one day soon he would believe in Your only Son so he also can have the eternal life you've given me. May the love and light of Christ shine in me so that he would be drawn closer to You.

The Power of Encouragement

My prayer is not that you take them out of the world
but that you protect them from the evil one.

JOHN 17:15

*E*very morning our kids get dressed and start the day. But no matter what they wear, they're not fully clothed until they put on the "outfit" they need to survive the battles ahead.

We wouldn't think of sending a soldier into war without the proper training and protective gear. In the same way, we need to equip our kids with the weapon of prayer as part of their full armor of God. Truth is, kids encounter a culture war every day. In our society, the lines between right and wrong have blurred to a confusing cloudiness. Values of faith and family are challenged in the schools, by friends, and in the media—on television, in music, on the Internet, everywhere.

Prayer releases the power of heaven to protect and defend our families. In Ephesians 6:11–12 we are told to "put on the full armor of God so that you can take your stand against the devil's schemes. For our struggle is not against flesh and blood, but against the rulers, against the authorities, against the powers of this dark world and against the spiritual forces of evil in the heavenly realms."

As Kim's two boys grew up, she prayed the full armor of God over Brandon and A.J. every morning before school.

What armor? The protective covering found in Ephesians 6:14–17: "Stand firm then, with the belt of truth buckled around your waist, with the breastplate of righteousness in place, and with your feet fitted with the readiness that comes from the gospel of peace. In addition to all this, take up the shield of faith, with which you can extinguish all the flaming arrows of the evil one. Take the helmet of salvation and the sword of the Spirit, which is the word of God."

Praying for your children—and encouraging them to pray—is one of the best gifts you can give them. And you can't begin too soon. Wendy and Steve pray with their young children before meals and at bedtime. One of the parents will first say, "Dear God," and the child will repeat that. Additional phrases are said and repeated until a short prayer is complete. It's not long or involved, but it's consistent. Children learn by seeing prayer modeled and by practicing it.

There's a familiar verse in Proverbs (22:6) that says, "Train a child in the way he should go, and when he is old he will not turn from it." We can encourage our children by praying both *with* them and *for* them.

Pray for your kids—and don't give up. Always remember what the Bible says: "The prayer of a righteous man [or woman] is powerful and effective" (James 5:16).

Love Your Kids

We love because he first loved us.
1 JOHN 4:19

*L*ord, I thank You for loving me and empowering me to love others. Help me to love my kids with words of affirmation and encouragement. Help me to make a priority of giving them my time and attention—to really listen to them, so they feel loved and valued. I pray for the wisdom to discipline in love, the energy to play, and the ability to laugh and enjoy my kids. Thank You for my children and Your love for all of us.

Encourage One Another

*Therefore encourage one another and build
each other up, just as in fact you are doing.*
1 THESSALONIANS 5:11

*L*ord, in our family, give us the grace to encourage one another. Help us to build each other up, not tear each other down. Help me to show approval to my children by catching them doing right, not just correcting when they do something wrong. Help me to give them what they need—whether it's a hug or a pat on the back, kind words or extra encouragement on a hard homework assignment. May I learn from You how to bring out the best in each of them.

Pray for Your Child's Salvation

*"I tell you the truth, anyone who will not receive the kingdom
of God like a little child will never enter it." And he took the
children in his arms, put his hands on them and blessed them.*
MARK 10:15–16

*L*ord, I ask and pray in the name and power of Jesus that You
would plant a seed in my child's heart to desire You. I pray she
would come to know You personally at a young age. Help her
to know You as her Savior and Lord and stay on the straight,
narrow path to Your kingdom. Give her ears to hear, eyes to
see, and a heart to receive Your love gift of salvation. Draw my
child to Yourself, I pray.

God's Armor of Protection

*Finally, be strong in the Lord and in his mighty power. Put on the
full armor of God so that you can take your stand against the devil's schemes.*
EPHESIANS 6:10–11

*L*ord, I thank You for Your protection of my children. With
the full armor of God, may they be strong in Your mighty
power. Help them to stand firm with the belt of truth and to
put on the breastplate of righteousness, knowing they are in
right standing with you. May the gospel of peace be like shoes
on their feet. As they take up the shield of faith, give them
the Holy Spirit to fight for victory over evil. With the helmet
of salvation and the sword of the Spirit—the actual Word of
God—may they be completely protected.

Teach Them to Pray

We will not hide them from their children; we will tell the next generation the praiseworthy deeds of the LORD, his power, and the wonders he has done. He decreed statutes for Jacob and established the law in Israel, which he commanded our forefathers to teach their children.

PSALM 78:4–5

Lord, I pray that You would help me to be a good role model as I teach my kids to pray. As a spiritual coach, empower me to pray *for* them and *with* them. May I provide clear instruction and a consistent example so my children can form good prayer habits. I know that I'm not perfect, but I am submitted to You. I ask that as I follow Your example, Lord, they will follow mine—and be people of prayer.

Love God and Know His Word

"Fix these words of mine in your hearts and minds; tie them as symbols on your hands and bind them on your foreheads. Teach them to your children, talking about them when you sit at home and when you walk along the road, when you lie down and when you get up."

DEUTERONOMY 11:18–19

*L*ord, it's essential that Your Word fill my heart and my children's. Help me to impress Your teachings on my kids by living what I believe. Help them to know the importance of Your ways as we talk about spiritual things—at home, in the car, or wherever we are living life. May we have the courage to share what You're doing in our lives and learn from each other. I pray that my family and I would live the Word daily because we know Your Word well.

Teach Them to Obey

Jesus replied, "If anyone loves me, he will obey my teaching. My Father will love him, and we will come to him and make our home with him."

JOHN 14:23

*L*ord, help my kids to love and obey You—and in doing so to obey me and my husband. Help them experience the joy of obedience, knowing that it pleases You and their parents and leads to blessing. As they learn to obey, give them cooperative and not rebellious spirits. And when they fail, choosing not to obey, please give me patience and the discernment to know how to discipline with love.

Prayer for a Newborn

*Yet you brought me out of the womb; you made me trust in you even
at my mother's breast. From birth I was cast upon you; from
my mother's womb you have been my God.*

PSALM 22:9–10

*L*ord, I prayed for this child, and You have granted me what
I asked. I thank You for the miracle of this new life. I pray
Your blessing on our precious baby. I pray for this child's
protection and safety. May our baby grow to be strong and
healthy in mind, soul, and spirit. Pour Your love and affection
into us, and help us to provide that same care and nurture in
our child's life. We commit this child to You, Lord. Please
bless our baby.

Prayer for Growing Children

*But grow in the grace and knowledge of our Lord and Savior Jesus Christ.
To him be glory both now and forever! Amen.*

2 PETER 3:18

*L*ord, as our children mature, I pray that they would come to
know You personally and grow in Your grace and knowledge.
May You bring glory to Your name as we help them to grow
up. Protect them and keep them in Your tender care as they
choose friends and learn to make decisions on their own.
Give them a hunger for You. Give them a desire for prayer.
Help them to have thankful and giving hearts.

Prayer for Teenagers

"This is what the LORD says to you: 'Do not be afraid or discouraged because of this vast army. For the battle is not yours, but God's.'"
2 CHRONICLES 20:15

*L*ord, I ask for wisdom and patience through my children's teenage years. As they navigate new waters of growth, replace their confusion with clear thinking. I pray for their self-control and the wisdom not to be swayed by their peers. Give them a passion for You and direction for life. May they be motivated and honest. Help me to connect with my kids at this age and seek to understand their world. I thank You that the battle is not mine to fight, but Yours, Lord.

Prayer for Other Children in My Life

Then little children were brought to Jesus for him to place his hands on them and pray for them. But the disciples rebuked those who brought them.
MATTHEW 19:13

*I*n my life, Lord, there are many children besides my own. I pray for them today. I lift up my children's friends; my nieces, nephews, and other relatives; my neighborhood children, foster children I know; and church kids. I ask that you would bless them all through me. So many children, Lord, need You. Show them Your love; reveal Your goodness and faithfulness to them. Bless their lives today, I pray.

For My Child's Life Mate

Do not arouse or awaken love until it so desires.
SONG OF SONGS 2:7

Lord, I pray for my children's future life partners today. Although they are only kids now, I pray for the spouses who will one day be their husbands or wives. Keep them pure and help them to wait for love. Bring into my children's lives spouses who are godly, loving, and supportive. I pray for mates who are well-suited for each other, who will seek to serve one another and live in harmony. I pray for Your will and Your timing on these vitally important life decisions.

Prayer for a Rebellious Child

Hear, O heavens! Listen, O earth! For the LORD has spoken:
"I reared children and brought them up, but they have rebelled against me."
ISAIAH 1:2

*P*lease, Lord, hear my prayer today for help. I need Your mighty power in my child's life. I pray against disobedience and defiance, and I ask that my rebellious child would return to obey both You and me. O God, I need You. Speak to my prodigal child and have mercy. I pray for restoration and forgiveness as Your gracious love revives this child's heart. Bring my child back to You and to our family again.

Bless Their Talents and Skills

Bless all his skills, O LORD, and be
pleased with the work of his hands.
DEUTERONOMY 33:11

*L*ord, as my children grow, I ask that You would bless their developing skills and abilities. May You be pleased with the work of their hearts, minds, and bodies. In their schoolwork, chores, and clubs and activities, may they do well and excel to the level of their abilities. Give them a desire to learn and grow with purpose and motivation in their chosen interests.

The Power of Harmony and Hospitality

*They broke bread in their homes
and ate together with glad and sincere hearts.*

ACTS 2:46

*O*nce upon a time there was a woman who loved God, worked vigorously, and took care of the needs of her family. She also reached out to the poor in her community. This woman was wise and made use of those teachable moments with her kids. And she did it all with strength, dignity, and a smile.

We don't know the woman's name, but we can read about her in Proverbs 31. While our twenty-first-century lives may be vastly different than this industrious woman's experience, certain essentials span the years. The core values of wisdom, faithfulness, dignity, strength, laughter, hard work, service to others, and preeminence of God first still hold as true today as they did some three thousand years ago. The Proverbs 31 woman was an excellent home manager, rewarded with praise from her husband, her kids, and others.

Whether you're married or single, working outside the home or not, one of your roles as a woman is being a household manager. When you are a wise steward of the resources God has provided, your home can become a place of blessing to all who enter. You create the "environment." Will it be a place of warmth and welcome—or an atmosphere of chaos and conflict?

Powerful things happen when you invite *God* to your house. When you call on this gracious Guest, He comes every time—and when He does, your home and family will never be the same. "If you are willing to invite God to involve himself in your daily challenges," says Bill Hybels, pastor of Willow Creek Church, "you will experience his prevailing power—in your home, in your relationships, in the marketplace, in the schools, in the church, wherever it is most needed. . . . God's prevailing power is released in the lives of people who pray."[4]

Prayer is foundational to every home—whether that's a mansion or a trailer, a cabin or a condo. You can pray power prayers throughout the day, in whatever part of your home you happen to be. Intercede for your husband while you're putting away laundry. Lift up your son's hard day at school while you make dinner. Thank God for the home you have and ask Him to help you wisely manage the resources He has provided.

Pray for protection and safety. Pray for more loving family relationships. Pray for more peace and harmony. Ask God to help your family better connect with Him and with each other—in spite of the busyness you all experience. Pray for a heart of hospitality to reach out to friends, neighbors, and your community as a whole.

A home that is built on love and fortified with prayer will stand strong and last long.

A Solid Foundation

*"Therefore everyone who hears these words of mine and
puts them into practice is like a wise man who
built his house on the rock."*
MATTHEW 7:24

*L*ord, I come before You to ask that You would establish our home on the solid rock of Your love. Please be our cornerstone. I pray that our family would be rooted in love, grounded in grace, and rich in respect for one another. Help us to be a family that reaches up to You, reaches in to support each other, and reaches out to the world around us. May we stand firm as a family built on a foundation of true faith.

Serve the Lord

*"But if serving the LORD seems undesirable to you, then choose
for yourselves this day whom you will serve.... But as for me
and my household, we will serve the LORD."*
JOSHUA 24:15

*L*ord, this world offers so many choices of things or people to whom we could give our allegiance. We will choose not to bow to the gods of materialism or selfishness. Instead, please give us the strength to serve You. As we humbly bow before You, we ask that You would provide for all our needs so we can be a means to help and supply the needs of others through our service and hospitality.

A Place of Love and Respect

Show proper respect to everyone: Love the brotherhood
of believers, fear God, honor the king.
1 PETER 2:17

*L*ord, may our home be a place where we show love and respect to each other. Help us to value each member of our family and everyone we welcome into our home. We may not always agree; we may have different opinions. But I pray that we would extend kindness to others and seek to view them as significant, worthy, and valuable. We choose to honor others in our home because we honor You.

Hospitality

Share with God's people who are in need.
Practice hospitality.
ROMANS 12:13

*L*ord, I thank You for my home. Show my heart opportunities to open this home to others. I want to share what You've provided for me. As I practice hospitality, may Your love shine through my life. However my home compares with others', I thank You for what I have. I am grateful that Your Spirit is present here. Give me a generous, open heart, and use my home for Your good purposes.

Living in Harmony

*They broke bread in their homes and ate
together with glad and sincere hearts.*
ACTS 2:46

*L*ord, may our home be a place of harmony. Let gladness and sincerity be hallmarks here as we share meals together, entertain, live, laugh, and play together as a family. I pray against discord and fighting, and I pray for peace. Give each of us an agreeable spirit. When the challenges of life come, help us to love and support each other with empathy, kindness, and love.

A Safe Place

My people will live in peaceful dwelling places,
in secure homes, in undisturbed places of rest.
ISAIAH 32:18

*L*ord, I ask that You would be our strong defense and protect our home. May this be a place of safety, comfort, and peace. Guard us from outside forces and protect us from harmful attacks from within. I pray that the Holy Spirit would put a hedge of protection around our home and family. Lord, we look to You as our refuge, our strength, and our security.

Encouraging Words

Pleasant words are a honeycomb, sweet to
the soul and healing to the bones.
PROVERBS 16:24

*L*ord, I pray that we would speak encouraging and kind words in our home. Help us to build each other up—never to tear each other down. Help us not to be so self-absorbed that we forget to ask how others around us are doing. Like honey, may the words from our mouths be sweet to the soul and healing to the bones. Help us to be positive, peaceable, and considerate. Thank You for giving us words that restore.

A Family That Prays Together

*He and all his family were devout and God-fearing;
he gave generously to those in need and prayed to God regularly.*
ACTS 10:2

*L*ord, I want our family to pray together more often. We need to put You first because You are the source of life—and You are worthy of our first fruits of time and attention. Help us make spending time with You a priority. I pray that meeting with You together will draw us closer to You and to each other. I believe You have so much more for us. I ask for Your blessing as we seek to honor You in this way.

Wise Stewardship

*The LORD is my strength and my shield; my heart trusts in him,
and I am helped. My heart leaps for joy and I will give thanks to him in song.*
PSALM 28:7

*L*ord, I thank You for the household You have entrusted to my care. Help me to be a wise steward of my resources, of all that You have provided. Help us to take care of our things, to keep them clean and in good repair. May we use our money wisely, may we share freely of Your blessings, and may we spend our time toward positive ends that bring glory to Your name.

Mentoring Other Women

*Likewise, teach the older women to be reverent in the way they live,
not to be slanderers or addicted to much wine, but to teach what is good.
Then they can train the younger women to love their husbands and children,
to be self-controlled and pure, to be busy at home, to be kind, and to be
subject to their husbands, so that no one will malign the word of God.*

TITUS 2:3–5

*L*ord, I thank You for the older women in my life who have been mentors to me. Whether they know it or not, women have counseled me with godly wisdom and taught me how to grow as a wife, as a mother, and as a woman. Teach me, Lord, to love my husband and children, to be self-controlled and pure, to be kind, and to know Your Word—so I can teach what is good to other women around me.

Family Celebrations

*These days should be remembered and observed in every generation
by every family, and in every province and in every city. And these days
of Purim should never cease to be celebrated by the Jews, nor should
the memory of them die out among their descendants.*

ESTHER 9:28

*L*ord, I thank You for the joy of celebration! Help us to be a family that remembers and gathers together—not just for birthdays and holidays, but even to celebrate the little blessings of life. As we laugh and play, eat and drink, challenge and encourage one another, we are thankful for all that You have done in our lives. May we have good memories of our family celebrations.

Blessing for a New House

The LORD's curse is on the house of the wicked,
but he blesses the home of the righteous.
PROVERBS 3:33

*L*ord, please bless this new house. We dedicate it to You in the name of Jesus. We ask that You would bring protection and safety to this place. Fill each room with Your loving presence, Your peace, and Your power. May we treat each other with respect and guests, with warmth and welcome. Use this house to bring glory to Your name, Lord. May all who come here feel at home.

Managing Your Household

*She watches over the affairs of her household
and does not eat the bread of idleness.*
PROVERBS 31:27

*L*ord, I thank You for the wisdom you give me each day to watch over the affairs of my household. Give me energy to accomplish my work and to keep our home organized and running smoothly. Help me to be a good time manager and to stay centered on Your purposes. I need to get my tasks done, but I also want to nurture and cherish my relationships. Empower me, Lord. Help our home to be a place of order, peace, and enjoyment.

Serve One Another in Love

*You, my brothers, were called to be free. But do not use your
freedom to indulge the sinful nature; rather, serve one another in love.*
GALATIANS 5:13

*L*ord, teach us how to serve one another. Whether I am preparing dinner, or my daughter is helping her sister rake the yard, or my husband and son are putting out the garbage, may each of us have the right motives. Help us, as we help others, to be loving and encouraging. Let us be more aware of the needs of others—and find delight in making their load easier. Help us to serve with a heart of love and gratitude.

The Power of Healing and Restoration

"Long life to you! Good health to you and your household!
And good health to all that is yours!"

1 SAMUEL 25:6

*H*ealth is one of our greatest God-given assets. "The healthier we are, the more stable our emotions," says Joyce Meyer in *Look Great, Feel Great*. "A healthy person can handle disappointments easier than one who is unhealthy. They can remain stable through the storms of life."[5] But though many of us understand that our body is a temple (1 Corinthians 6:19), we often treat it more like a trash can. Are we really taking care of ourselves when we eat junk food, avoid exercise, and fill our minds with the negativity of today's entertainment?

We can pray powerful and effective prayers for health, healing, and wholeness, in our lives and in the lives of others, when we

- *pray boldly:* "Let us then approach the throne of grace with confidence, so that we may receive mercy and find grace to help us in our time of need" (Hebrews 4:16);
- *ask in Jesus' name*: "Until now you have not asked for anything in my name. Ask and you will receive, and

71

your joy will be complete" (John 16:24);
- *pray in faith:* "If you believe, you will receive whatever you ask for in prayer" (Matthew 21:22).

Faith and prayer go together. Martin Luther said, "Faith makes the prayer acceptable because it believes that either the prayer will be answered, or that something better will be given instead."[6]

When we pray, we release the power of heaven into our lives. But there are times when our prayers for healing are not answered with a "yes." How do we cope—and what can we learn? In his classic book *Prayer*, George A. Buttrick says, "True prayer does not evade pain, but gains from it insight, patience, courage, and sympathy. . . . This is healing beyond healing. By this prayer we are 'more than conquerors': the realism of unanswered prayer becomes the very Presence of God."[7]

Mary Ann provides a good example of this. Diagnosed with multiple sclerosis at age twenty-seven, she was soon debilitated—but then, surprisingly, the disease went into remission for several years. When her youngest daughter left for college, Mary Ann's health quickly declined again, and she was confined to a wheelchair for the rest of her life.

Early on, Mary Ann had prayed, "God, please let me be well enough to raise my girls." It was by His grace that her disease was in remission all the years her children were growing up. Mary Ann's daughter marvels at the fact that her mother never complained about the unfairness of MS— she accepted the life God gave her and used the resources she had to beautifully represent her Lord. When Mary Ann died at age sixty-five, scores of people attended a memorial service to give thanks for her encouraging example.

When God heals, we praise Him. When He does not, we praise Him still. Either way, we are changed within.

For Good Health

Say to him: "Long life to you! Good health to you
and your household! And good health to all that is yours!"

1 SAMUEL 25:6

*L*ord, I thank You for my good health. It is a blessing. I pray for Your power to sustain me as I take care of myself—by eating healthy food, drinking enough water, and making movement and exercise a part of my daily life. Give me the self-control and motivation I need to make wise choices to support the health of my mind, my spirit, and my body. Please keep me from injury and illness, and keep me safe, I pray.

For a Positive Attitude

A cheerful look brings joy to the heart, and good
news gives health to the bones.

PROVERBS 15:30

*L*ord, I want a more cheerful outlook on life. I pray for a hopeful disposition. When I tend toward negativity and cynicism, I know you can heal me. Please help me to live with real joy, not just a pasted-on smile. As I spend more time with You, may Your joy flow through me. And, Lord, may I bring joy to the hearts of others.

Spiritual Health

The LORD is my shepherd, I shall not be in want. He makes me lie down in green pastures, he leads me beside quiet waters, he restores my soul. He guides me in paths of righteousness for his name's sake. Even though I walk through the valley of the shadow of death, I will fear no evil, for you are with me; your rod and your staff, they comfort me. You prepare a table before me in the presence of my enemies. You anoint my head with oil; my cup overflows. Surely goodness and love will follow me all the days of my life, and I will dwell in the house of the LORD forever.

PSALM 23

*L*ord, I need Your times of refreshing in my life. Bread of Heaven, as You nourish my body with food, feed my soul with Your words of comfort and life. May I be filled with Your healing love, joy, and goodness. I praise You, Father, for providing green pastures, places to relax and unwind in the Spirit. Please still my heart from distractions and be the restorer of my soul.

Wholeness and Right Living

Do not be wise in your own eyes; fear the LORD and shun evil. This will bring health to your body and nourishment to your bones.

PROVERBS 3:7–8

*L*ord, help me to be a person who takes care of herself. As I look to Your wisdom for right living, may I enjoy a healthy body. I need to take responsibility for my actions—what I choose to put in my mouth and my mind is up to me. Help me to make wise decisions and to be a good steward of myself, the "temple" You have given me. Help me not to abuse my body, but to care for it as You would want me to.

Getting Rid of Stress

Cast all your anxiety on him because he cares for you.
1 PETER 5:7

*L*ord, help me to find relief from stress in my life. I need to value rest and make time to relax—and I need Your power to do so. I cast my cares on You, my burden bearer. Help me to deal with the toxic, unhealthy relationships in my life. Give me the strength to say no when I need better emotional boundaries. And please help me find joy again in the things I like to do—unwinding with music, taking a walk, calling a friend, or learning a new hobby. Calm me and renew me, Lord.

Rest for the Weary

"Come to me, all you who are weary and burdened, and I will give you rest. Take my yoke upon you and learn from me, for I am gentle and humble in heart, and you will find rest for your souls. For my yoke is easy and my burden is light."

MATTHEW 11:28–30

*L*ord, I need rest. I am so tired and worn-out. I pray that I will sleep well at night. I ask for more energy during the day and a more vibrant spirit. Lighten my load so I can have a better balance among my work, my ministry, and my home life. Replenish me, Lord. As I unwind in spirit and body, please fill me with peace and rest.

Time and Motivation for Fitness

Do you not know that your body is a temple of the Holy Spirit, who is in you, whom you have received from God? You are not your own; you were bought at a price. Therefore honor God with your body.

1 CORINTHIANS 6:19–20

*L*ord, I need more time—and motivation—to get in shape. I want to have a fitness routine, but my schedule is crazy; there is always so much to do every day. Show me how to make movement a priority in my life so I will feel better, look better, and have more energy. I want to honor You with my body in my physical health. Lord, I want to be a woman of balance, not extremes. Help me to care for my body and be a wise steward of this resource You've given me all the days of my life.

Eating Right

Go, eat your food with gladness, and drink your wine
with a joyful heart, for it is now that God favors what you do.
ECCLESIASTES 9:7

*L*ord, I thank You for filling the earth with a bounty of food. I praise You for the variety of fruits, vegetables, proteins, and carbohydrates you provide for sustaining life. Help me to make a priority of eating a nutritious blend of foods, to drink enough water, and to avoid overindulging in junk. I pray for the time to shop and cook balanced meals. Please help me find food that is healthy and good-tasting, and the will to eat in moderation.

Keeping Your Mind Active

So then, let us not be like others, who are asleep,
but let us be alert and self-controlled.
1 THESSALONIANS 5:6

*L*ord, I want to keep my mind healthy and active. Give me wisdom regarding what I put into my mind. I need to feed it the right things so I can be alert and self-controlled. Keep me from watching mind-polluting junk on television or at the movies. Open my mind to healthy pursuits that challenge my thinking, grow good thoughts, and help me to be a wiser, godlier person.

Good Emotional Health

Such confidence as this is ours through Christ before God. Not that
we are competent in ourselves to claim anything for ourselves,
but our competence comes from God.

2 CORINTHIANS 3:4–5

*L*ord, I thank You for all the emotions we have. Help me to enjoy stable and good emotional health. I pray for wholeness in my feelings. I pray that I would have more confidence, and that I would find my competence in You. I ask for healthier self-esteem—that I would know my true worth and find my value in who I am in Christ. I pray for more laughter, fun, and play in my life. Thank You for caring about all aspects of my health—my mind, my emotions, and my body.

A Clean Environment

How can a young man keep his way pure? By living according to your word.
I seek you with all my heart; do not let me stray from your commands. I have hidden
your word in my heart that I might not sin against you.

PSALM 119:9–11

*L*ord, I want to live a clean, healthy life. As I abide in Your Word, help me to be pure in my thought life and in my body. Help me provide a healthy environment in my home with less dirt and dust and fewer germs. And I pray that, outside my home, people will work together to lessen pollution so we can all breathe cleaner air and drink better water. In our city, in our home, in our bodies, Lord, help us to live healthy in cleaner environments.

Prayer for Healing

This was to fulfill what was spoken through the prophet Isaiah: "He took up our infirmities and carried our diseases."
MATTHEW 8:17

Lord God, my healer, I ask in the name of Jesus that You would relieve my injury or illness today. By Your wounds, Lord, I am healed. I ask that You would relieve my pain and suffering. Show the doctors how to best help me. Touch me with Your power and Your presence. I humbly ask You to make me well. And if You choose not to, Lord, help me to praise You anyway, looking for the good purpose You have in my life. Your will be done, Father.

Living with Pain

Great is the LORD and most worthy of praise;
his greatness no one can fathom.

PSALM 145:3

*L*ord, I choose to praise You through this pain. You are great, and there is no one worthy of Your honor and glory. "Heal me, O LORD, and I will be healed; save me and I will be saved, for you are the One I praise" (Jeremiah 17:14). I give you this discomfort, and I ask in the name and power of Jesus that You would take it away. Help me and heal me completely from my hurt. Let my heart ache only for the comfort and healing balm of Your presence.

When Healing Does Not Come

I consider that our present sufferings are not worth comparing with the glory that will
be revealed in us. . . . And we know that in all things God works for the good of those
who love him, who have been called according to his purpose.

ROMANS 8:18, 28

*L*ord, I have prayed, and healing hasn't come. It's hard to know why You do not heal when You clearly have the power to do so. Please help me not to focus on my present suffering, but to be transformed in my attitude. May I revel in the glory that will be revealed in me through this and, ultimately, when I am with You in heaven. I do not understand, but I choose to praise You anyway. Give me the peace, comfort, and assurance that all things, even this, will work for my good and for Your glory.

The Power of Obedience

But may the righteous be glad and rejoice before God;
may they be happy and joyful.

PSALM 68:3

Where does joy come from? From winning a trip to Hawaii? Is it in the bliss of a newborn baby? Or maybe from the calm delight of watching a sunset with the one you love? Those things may bring us happiness, but what happens when it rains at the beach, the baby has colic, or the one you love no longer wants to watch sunsets with you?

True joy is not fleeting nor dependent on our circumstances. Though the world may seem intent on squelching our happiness, we can learn to pray powerfully for more *joy* in our lives. It starts with asking.

"This is the confidence we have in approaching God," the apostle John wrote in 1 John 5:14–15, "that if we ask anything according to his will, he hears us. And if we know that he hears us—whatever we ask—we know that we have what we asked of him."

Of course, the timing is God's prerogative. A woman named Sarah knew that God answers prayer, but she wasn't willing to wait on Him. She wanted a son, and in spite of God's promise to her husband, Abraham, she tried to arrange for the baby's birth by a surrogate, her servant Hagar. Hagar's son, Ishmael, caused much grief to Sarah—

but God was gracious and ultimately provided Sarah and Abraham the son, Isaac, He had promised long before. "God has brought me laughter, and everyone who hears about this will laugh with me," Sarah said finally (Genesis 21:6).

In surrendering our will for God's will and following His commands, we can realize more of God's power and joy in our lives. Jesus said, "If you obey my commands, you will remain in my love, just as I have obeyed my Father's commands and remain in his love. I have told you this so that my joy may be in you and that your joy may be complete" (John 15:9–11).

A heart full of joy is a heart that sings praise and thanks to God. Praising Him multiplies our joy and increases our faith. "Praise is the spark plug of faith," says Kay Arthur in *When Bad Things Happen*. "Praise gets faith airborne, where it can soar above the gravitational forces of this world's cares. The secret of faith is continual praise even when your inward parts tremble, lips quiver, and decay enters your bones."[8]

Praising and thanking God—for who He is and all He has done—will make any hard day better. "The LORD is my strength and my shield," the psalmist wrote. "My heart trusts in him, and I am helped. My heart leaps for joy and I will give thanks to him in song" (Psalm 28:7).

Finding Strength

*"Go and enjoy choice food and sweet drinks, and send some to
those who have nothing prepared. This day is sacred to our Lord.
Do not grieve, for the joy of the LORD is your strength."*

NEHEMIAH 8:10

*L*ord, I am tired and weary. Infuse me with life, energy, and
joy again. I thank You for being my strength and my delight. I
don't have to look to a bowl of ice cream or the compliments of
a friend to fill me up on the inside. Steady and constant, You
are my source; You are the One who fills me. Sustain me, Lord,
with the power of Your love, so I can live my life refreshed and
renewed.

Joy Despite Trials

*Consider it pure joy, my brothers, whenever you face trials of many kinds,
because you know that the testing of your faith develops perseverance. Perseverance
must finish its work so that you may be mature and complete, not lacking anything.
If any of you lacks wisdom, he should ask God, who gives generously to all without
finding fault, and it will be given to him.*

JAMES 1:2–5

*L*ord, it seems odd to consider trials a joyful thing. But I pray
that my challenges in life, these times of testing, will lead me to
greater perseverance. May that perseverance finish its work so I
will be mature and complete, on my way to wholeness. I ask for
wisdom and Your perspective as I seek joy in life's challenges—
and the better times that will come my way.

Joyful in Hope

Be joyful in hope, patient in affliction, faithful in prayer.
ROMANS 12:12

*L*ord, I thank You for giving me hope. I don't know where I would be without You. I don't know what the future holds, but You give me the ability to be joyful even while I wait—even when I don't understand. Please help me to have a positive attitude and live with a mind-set of patience and courage as You work Your will in my life. Help me to remain faithful in prayer, Lord, and fully committed to You.

The Joy of Knowing Jesus

*Restore to me the joy of your salvation and
grant me a willing spirit, to sustain me.*
PSALM 51:12

*J*esus, knowing You brings me joy! I am so glad that I am saved and on my way to heaven. Thank You for the abundant life You provide. I can smile because I know that You love me. I can be positive because You have the power to heal, restore, and revive. Your presence brings me joy—just being with You is such a privilege. You are awesome, and I delight to know You and tell others about You.

Joy in God's Protection

But let all who take refuge in you be glad; let them ever sing for joy. Spread your
protection over them, that those who love your name may rejoice in you.
PSALM 5:11

*L*ord, please cover me. Protect me from my enemies—fear and doubt, worry and human reasoning. I try to figure everything out, but I end up confused and tired. Let me rest in the comfort of Your love and the safety of Your protection. Here, abiding in You, I am secure and I am glad. Spread Your consolation over me as I rejoice in You. You are my joy and my protection, Lord.

I Need More Joy

Splendor and majesty are before him;
strength and joy in his dwelling place.
1 CHRONICLES 16:27

*L*ord, buoy my spirits. I need more joy in my life. Daily living and trials can be so depleting; I just can't do it on my own. Help me to laugh more and enjoy life again. Help me to have a childlike, playful spirit—a lighter heart, Lord. Encourage me so I can bless others with a kind word or a smile. Let me come to Your dwelling place and find strength and joy in praising You. In Your presence is fullness of joy!

Real and Lasting Joy

For the kingdom of God is not a matter of eating and drinking,
but of righteousness, peace and joy in the Holy Spirit.
ROMANS 14:17

*L*ord, I am so tired of imitations. People pretend to be something they're not. Food is flavored with artificial ingredients. It's hard to tell what is false and what is true anymore. When it comes to joy, I want the real thing. Pour into my life Your genuine and lasting joy. I need more of You, Lord. I pray for righteousness, peace, and joy in the Holy Spirit. Fill me, please.

Joy in Praying for Others

In all my prayers for all of you, I always pray with joy.
PHILIPPIANS 1:4

*L*ord, I thank You for the joy and privilege of praying for others. What a blessing to be able to intercede, to stand in the gap and move heaven and earth for those I love. In all my prayers for those I know, may I have a heart of joy. Bless my family and friends, Lord. Bless those who need You today. May I find satisfaction in lifting up prayers for others.

The Delight of Answered Prayer

"Until now you have not asked for anything in my name.
Ask and you will receive, and your joy will be complete."
JOHN 16:24

*L*ord, I thank You for the joy of answered prayer! You are amazing. I delight in You and thank You with a full heart. I asked and You answered. I receive what You give with a grateful heart. Lord, You are good. You are faithful. You are my joy and my delight. I praise Your holy name. I am smiling at You right now. Thank You for filling my heart with gladness, Lord.

Finding Joy in God's Presence

*"You have made known to me the paths of life; you will
fill me with joy in your presence."*

ACTS 2:28

*L*ord, draw me closer to You. In Your presence is fullness of joy—and I want to be filled. Knowing I am loved by You makes me glad; I cannot imagine life without You. With You there is light; without You, darkness. With You there is pleasure; without You, pain. You care, You comfort; You really listen. Here, in Your presence, I am loved, I am renewed, and I am very happy.

Enjoying God's Blessings

*The LORD has done great things for us,
and we are filled with joy.*

PSALM 126:3

*L*ord, I thank You for the work of Your hands. A wildflower, a mountain scene, the ocean waves on a white sand beach— the beauty of the earth reveals Your glory. Thank You for the smile of a child, the touch of my beloved's hand, the warmth of our home. I am grateful for the love of friends and meaningful work. You have done great things for us, and we are filled with joy. Thank You for Your many blessings.

Living Daily with Delight

You will go out in joy and be led forth in peace; the mountains and hills will burst into song before you, and all the trees of the field will clap their hands.
ISAIAH 55:12

*L*ord, I thank You for the joy You bring every day. Whether I go out or stay in, joy is with me—because You are there. Lead me forth today in peace. May all of creation—even the trees of the field—praise You as I as praise You. Help me to live with a lighter heart and a positive attitude despite the distractions and duties that seek to steal my joy. I choose You. Help me to live daily with Your delight.

Obedience Leads to Joy

"As the Father has loved me, so have I loved you. Now remain in my love.
If you obey my commands, you will remain in my love, just as I have
obeyed my Father's commands and remain in his love. I have told
you this so that my joy may be in you and that your joy may be complete."

JOHN 15:9–11

*L*ord, Your Word says that if we obey Your commands, we will remain in Your love. I want to serve You out of an obedient, not a rebellious, heart. Just as Jesus submits to You, Father, I choose to submit to You, too. Obedience leads to a blessing. Empower me, encourage me, and give me the will to want to make right decisions, decisions that lead to a better life and greater joy.

Your Reward Will Come

Therefore, since we are surrounded by such a great cloud of witnesses,
let us throw off everything that hinders and the sin that so easily entangles,
and let us run with perseverance the race marked out for us. Let us fix our
eyes on Jesus, the author and perfecter of our faith, who for the joy set
before him endured the cross, scorning its shame, and sat down at the
right hand of the throne of God. Consider him who endured such opposition
from sinful men, so that you will not grow weary and lose heart.

HEBREWS 12:1–3

*L*ord, sometimes I get worn out and weary. I work hard; I try to do the right thing. But I lose focus. Help me to fix my eyes on *Your* power not *my* circumstances. Lift me up, and help me to remember the joy of the reward to come. I pray for perseverance as I consider the joy of the prize: I get to be with You forever in heaven. Free of pain, full of joy. Refresh me with Your truth, O Lord.

The Power of Contentment

"The LORD bless you and keep you;
the LORD make his face shine upon you and be gracious to you;
the LORD turn his face toward you and give you peace."

NUMBERS 6:24–26

*A*s I write this, it's snowing. A blizzard, actually. Although it's only late October, the winds are whipping and fourteen inches of snow are piling up on the lawn and lawn furniture. Inside the house, though, all is calm—because the sturdy walls protect me from the stormy blast. Content and safe by a warm fireplace, I am at peace.

Like a winter squall, the storms of life can threaten our inner peace. An unexpected job layoff or doctor's report can disrupt our emotional equilibrium. A hurtful comment from a neighbor or coworker can cut us to the core. Even the daily duties of life—from diapers and dishes to deals and deadlines—leave us exhausted.

For most of us, life is busy—and the peace we find often seems short-lived. There is so much to think about— the kids, the mortgage, our health, and how we're ever going to find time to get everything done. Even contentment, when we find it, is fleeting. We get our dream jobs, our husbands surprise us with special vacations, our adult children finally find their own places to live. But with the flip of a calendar page, discontentment returns.

Why is peace so elusive? Perhaps because we forget to pray and replenish our source of peace. We can find lasting contentment in Christ, regardless of our circumstances, when we come to the One who calms the storms. "It is in the silence of the heart that God speaks," said Mother Teresa[9]—but too often our hearts are neither still nor silent.

Peace rarely comes naturally; in most cases, we need to learn it. The true story of two sisters provides a good example: Mary, Martha, and their brother Lazarus (yes, the same guy Jesus raised from the dead) all lived in the town of Bethany. When Jesus came to visit, Martha scurried around preparing food while Mary took to the opportunity to sit at Jesus' feet and absorb the enlightening things He said. That day, Mary made the better choice, because Jesus would not be with them much longer. She had been wise and was rewarded for it. (You can read the whole story in Luke 10:38–41.)

In the midst of a frenzied life, though, we can find a refuge, a sanctuary of inner stillness, in drawing near to God. Powerful prayers for peace rise as we spend time in His presence, enjoying and resting in His capable strength. Just as the moon takes its light and power from the sun, we can bask in the glow of God's Son and absorb His truth. Then we'll be women who reflect His joy and light the dark corners of the world around us. Peace is possible when we seek the source of peace through prayer.

Jesus, Prince of Peace

*For to us a child is born, to us a son is given, and the government
will be on his shoulders. And he will be called Wonderful Counselor,
Mighty God, Everlasting Father, Prince of Peace.*

ISAIAH 9:6

*L*ord, I thank You that I can have a calm spirit—because You are the Prince of Peace. Your name, Jesus, has the authority to make fear and worry flee. Your name has power! You are called Wonderful Counselor because You freely give wisdom and guidance. You are the Mighty God, the One who made the entire world and keeps it all going. My Everlasting Father, it's Your love and compassion that sustain me. My Prince of Peace, I worship and honor You.

Be a Peacemaker

*Blessed are the peacemakers, for
they will be called sons of God.*

MATTHEW 5:9

*L*ord, please make me a tool of Your peace. Instead of the hammer of judgment, let me bring balm of love. Instead of bitterness and resentment, help me to quickly forgive. When doubt misaligns my emotions, level me with faith. When I cannot find an answer, let me know Your great hope. When I cannot see the way, bring Your light to my darkness. When I am feeling low, bring me joy. Lord, let me receive all these things so I can console others and be a peacemaker. (Inspired by the prayer of St. Francis.)

Calm My Anxious Heart

*Do not be anxious about anything, but in everything, by prayer
and petition, with thanksgiving, present your requests to God.
And the peace of God, which transcends all understanding,
will guard your hearts and your minds in Christ Jesus.*
PHILIPPIANS 4:6–7

*L*ord, I don't want to be anxious about anything, but so often
I am. I thank You that You understand. Right now, I release
my burdens and cares to You. I give You my heavy heart and
my flailing emotions. I ask that You calm me, despite all
that is happening in my life. As I keep my thoughts, actions,
and attitudes centered on Jesus, Your peace comes. I thank
You for Your peace that settles on me even when I do not
understand.

We Are Overcomers

*"I have told you these things, so that in
me you may have peace. In this world you will
have trouble. But take heart! I have overcome the world."*
JOHN 16:33

*L*ord, our world is filled with trouble and pain—from the
abuse, crime, and terrorism I see on the news to the drug abuse,
affairs, and pornography addictions I hear about from people
I know. Sometimes it seems like too much to handle. I am so
glad that I have You, Lord. In this world there is trouble, but
with You—being connected to You—I can have peace.

Finding Contentment

Godliness with contentment is great gain.
1 TIMOTHY 6:6

*L*ord, please help me to find my contentment in You. I don't want to be defined by "stuff"—the things I own or what I do. May my greatest happiness in life be knowing who You are and who I am in Christ. May I treasure the simple things in life, those things that bring me peace. With Your grace, I rest secure. Like Mary, I choose to sit at Your feet. You, Lord, are my satisfaction.

The Peace That Brings Life

A heart at peace gives life to the body, but envy rots the bones.
PROVERBS 14:30

*L*ord, I thank You for the peace that restores me mentally, emotionally, and physically. It is the peace that brings wholeness. When my heart is restless, my health suffers. But when I am at peace, You restore my entire body. I can breathe easier, I can relax, and I can smile again because I know everything's going to be all right. You are in control. I thank You that Your peace brings life.

A Peaceful Life

. . .that we may live peaceful and quiet lives in all godliness and holiness.
1 TIMOTHY 2:2

*L*ord, I don't want peace to be a once-in-a-while thing—I want to know peace as a way of life. Make me a conduit that brings harmony and serenity to all my relationships and interactions. Even when life is busy, I want to be a person who takes time to listen to others. Still my inner heart so I can give a smile or a kind word to another person and, through my actions, offer peace to them as well.

The Wisdom of Peace

But the wisdom that comes from heaven is first of all pure; then peace-loving,
considerate, submissive, full of mercy and good fruit, impartial and sincere.
Peacemakers who sow in peace raise a harvest of righteousness.
JAMES 3:17–18

*L*ord, please plant Your wisdom in me like seeds in the soil. Each one is a gift from heaven. Help me cultivate each one and learn to follow Your ways. They are pure, peace-loving, considerate, submissive, full of mercy and good fruit, impartial, and sincere. May I be a person who sows in peace and raises a harvest of righteousness. As I look to Your Word for growth, teach me to meditate on it and apply it to my life.

Where Is Peace Found?

For the kingdom of God is not a matter of eating and drinking,
but of righteousness, peace and joy in the Holy Spirit, because anyone
who serves Christ in this way is pleasing to God and approved by men.
ROMANS 14:17–18

*L*ord, everyone is looking for peace. Some travel to other countries or try alternative philosophies and lifestyles to find an inner tranquillity. Some think food or wine will satisfy the hole in the heart that only You can fill. But Your Word tells us it's not what we eat or drink that provides lasting satisfaction. May I find peace and joy in Your Holy Spirit, Lord. Knowing You, loving You, and experiencing You is true peace. Thank You, Lord.

A Blessing of Peace

"The LORD bless you and keep you; the LORD make his face
shine upon you and be gracious to you; the LORD turn his
face toward you and give you peace."
NUMBERS 6:24–26

*L*ord, long ago You told Moses to have Aaron and his sons bless the Israelites with these words. I ask that You would bless me with peace as I pray: "The LORD bless you and keep you; the LORD make his face shine upon you and be gracious to you; the LORD turn his face toward you and give you peace." Turn to me, and let Your love and mercy shine on me so I can be a light that shines the way for others.

Focus on God, Not Circumstances

You will keep in perfect peace him whose
mind is steadfast, because he trusts in you.
ISAIAH 26:3

*L*ord, so many times it seems as if a thief is trying to steal my peace. My circumstances can be overwhelming—and they shake me up. I don't want to be robbed of happiness and emotional stability. I ask that You would keep me in perfect peace as I choose to put my eyes on You rather than on my problems. Let my mind be steady, not racing. Let my heart trust that You will see me through.

Peace Like a River

If only you had paid attention to my commands, your peace would have been like a river, your righteousness like the waves of the sea.
ISAIAH 48:18

*L*ord, I need Your river of life to flow through me today. Wash away my cares and help me to follow as I learn to "go with the flow" of Your will. Still my restless heart with the grandeur of Your creation. I can imagine myself walking on a sandy shore, the ocean mist and rhythmic music of the waves revealing Your splendor. I appreciate all You have made. I thank You for the peace Your creation brings.

Learning the Ways of Peace

. . .to be peaceable and considerate, and to
show true humility toward all men.

TITUS 3:2

*L*ord, I am so grateful that You are helping me become a person who walks in peace. Mentor me in Your ways so I can live in harmony and be a positive example for others.I don't want to put anyone down; I want to build them up. I don't want to start fights or nag people; I want to bring them happiness. Instead of putting myself first, let me be considerate of others. Forgive me if I have been proud or arrogant; teach me, Lord, to be humble.

Not as the World Gives

"Peace I leave with you; my peace I give you. I do not give to you as the world gives.
Do not let your hearts be troubled and do not be afraid."

JOHN 14:27

*L*ord, Your peace is unlike anything that the world offers. I don't need to upgrade to a new model every year—there's no "Peace 5.0" to download. I have the only version I need when I have Your peace, whether that's a calm tranquillity, a quiet stillness, or the inner knowledge that everything's going to be all right. I value my right standing with You and the harmony that brings to my relationships. Your peace is real and lasting, never to be taken away.

The Power of Faith

Courage is fear that has said its prayers.
JILL BRISCOE

I was terrified the first time I drove a car in England. Suddenly, I had to put aside everything I had learned about the right and wrong sides of the road. In the United States, we drive on the right—but in that country left is right. Everything is opposite.

Feeling as if the other cars were going to hit me, I drove slower than usual. That is, until my brother-in-law said firmly, "Steel your nerves and press on!" I was afraid, but I did what he said, praying silently, "Lord, help me do this." Finally, we completed a safe trip to our destination, and I felt a great sense of accomplishment. With the Lord's help, I had faced and conquered my fear.

Fear has many sources. When our safety is threatened, we are rightly afraid because we don't know what will happen. Our bodies are equipped with an inner alarm to signal "something is not right," in order to protect us from harm. But we need wisdom to discern real fear from false. If we hear an unfamiliar noise in the middle of the night, for instance, we may be afraid. But once we discover it's only the wind blowing branches against a windowpane, our minds can rest again.

The list of fears is endless. Melanie doesn't want to travel because she's afraid of flying. Sandra worries her son will be injured playing football. LaTrisha has dated one too many losers and fears being alone the rest of her life. Many people dread what other people may think of them. Some are afraid of making mistakes. From a fear of the dark to the horror of public speaking, many people live in trepidation. But it doesn't have to be that way.

When the Lord called Moses to free the Israelites from the slavery of Egypt, the former shepherd was very much afraid. Moses felt totally unqualified for the job, but God said to him, "I have raised you up for this very purpose, *that I might show you my power* and that my name might be proclaimed in all the earth" (Exodus 9:16, emphasis added). When we fear we're not good enough, we are looking only at our own limited abilities instead of at God's unlimited power and resources.

Praying effective prayers over our fears begins as we release those fears to God and ask Him for a heart of faith. What brings us to that point? Trust. Faith and trust overcome fear when we discover the depth of God's heart of love—and believe that He is not only capable, but more than willing, to help us in our times of need. As the apostle Paul wrote, "I know whom I have believed, and am convinced that he is able to guard what I have entrusted to him for that day" (2 Timothy 1:12).

No Doubt

But when he asks, he must believe and not doubt, because
he who doubts is like a wave of the sea, blown and tossed by the wind.

JAMES 1:6

*L*ord, rescue me from my sea of doubt and fear. I have lived with uncertainty and suspicion for too long. I don't want to be like an ocean wave that is blown and tossed by the wind. I ask that You would quiet my stormy emotions and help me believe that You will take care of me. When I'm tempted to be cynical, help me choose to step away from fear and closer to faith.

Safe in Danger

For in the day of trouble he will keep me safe in his dwelling;
he will hide me in the shelter of his tabernacle and set me high upon a rock.

PSALM 27:5

*L*ord, I need Your protection. Keep me safe in Your dwelling place. Hide me from my enemies in Your secure shelter. Comfort me with Your warm blanket of peace and love. I am safe with You, and in Your protection—in Your presence—I can move from fearful to fearless, from timid to trusting. Here, Lord, I am safe from harm.

Light in My Darkness

The LORD is my light and my salvation—whom shall I fear?
The LORD is the stronghold of my life—of whom shall I be afraid?
PSALM 27:1

*L*ord, often I am afraid. In the dark, challenging times of my life I can't always see the way. I don't know what to do or where to go. But You are light! I thank You that You can see in the dark—the darkness is as light to You—so I don't have to be afraid. When my enemies try to ruin my life, they don't stand a chance, Lord. You save me. No matter what happens, I will be confident in You.

No Fear in Love

There is no fear in love. But perfect love drives out fear,
because fear has to do with punishment. The One
who fears is not made perfect in love.
1 JOHN 4:18

*L*ord, I thank You that Your great love conquers fear! I can love people freely because You live in me. It doesn't have to be scary to reveal my inner self. I don't have to fear rejection. I may be accepted or not, but either way I can love with confidence because Your perfect love drives out fear. Give me the courage to live that life of love.

God Strengthens You

So do not fear, for I am with you; do not be dismayed,
for I am your God. I will strengthen you and help you;
I will uphold you with my righteous right hand.
ISAIAH 41:10

*L*ord, I need Your strength in me. Stronger than steel, Your character is so solid I don't have to be afraid. You are with me—and that means everything. I can have joy because of Your joy in me. With Your righteous right hand you help me, deliver me, and uphold me. As You take my hand and say, "Do not fear, I will help you," I smile in gratitude and thanks.

Power, Love, and Self Discipline

*For God did not give us a spirit of timidity, but a
spirit of power, of love and of self-discipline.*
2 TIMOTHY 1:7

*L*ord, You give me many good gifts—but I know that fear is not one of them. Fear is not from You. Graciously, You have provided for me a spirit of power, love, and self-discipline—power to do Your will, power to love others (even when I don't feel like it), and the power to discipline myself to think about things that lead me into faith rather than fear.

Do Not Fear Man

*Fear of man will prove to be a snare, but
whoever trusts in the LORD is kept safe.*
PROVERBS 29:25

*L*ord, I have looked for approval from men for too long. That's a snare, a trap for my emotions. I long for the acceptance of other people—and am more often than not disappointed. My fears have gotten in the way. Forgive me, Lord. I want to trust in You. Keep me safe and deliver me from this hunger for human approval. Bring me into the freedom of Your grace.

God Will Save You

*Strengthen the feeble hands, steady the knees that give way; say to those with fearful
hearts, "Be strong, do not fear; your God will come, he will come with vengeance; with
divine retribution he will come to save you."*

ISAIAH 35:3–4

*L*ord, steady me. Strengthen the emotional muscle of my heart so that I am not so fearful all the time. I want to be stronger. I want to have more faith. I choose to believe in the One who knows everything and has the power to change hearts and lives. My God will come. My God will save me and take care of the ones who have hurt me. I watch and pray for Your justice, Lord.

God Is More Than Able

*I know whom I have believed, and am convinced that
he is able to guard what I have entrusted to him for that day.*

2 TIMOTHY 1:12

*L*ord, I am so grateful that I know You—and I am learning more about Your character every day. You are holy and sovereign and righteous and just. You are loving and faithful and always good. When I know the One I believe and have a strong conviction that He is willing and able to help me, I can have more peace. You *want* to help me! My God will take care of me. Thank You, Lord.

God's Power to Conquer Fear

"But I have raised you up for this very purpose, that I
might show you my power and that my name
might be proclaimed in all the earth."

EXODUS 9:16

*L*ord, You never give in to defeat. You are a strong conqueror of sin and evil. I need Your authority and influence to muscle fear out of my life. You called Moses to lead the Israelites from slavery to freedom. Lead me from my own personal bondage to walk in freedom and peace. Show Your power in my life and let Your name be lifted up. You get the credit, Lord—let everyone know what You have done to change me.

No Fear of Disgrace

"Do not be afraid; you will not suffer shame. Do not fear disgrace;
you will not be humiliated. You will forget the shame of your
youth and remember no more the reproach of your widowhood.
For your Maker is your husband—the LORD Almighty is his name—the
Holy One of Israel is your Redeemer; he is called the God of all the earth.

ISAIAH 54:4–5

*L*ord, it's hard for me to admit this, but at times I feel so humiliated. Other people have caused me great pain. Throughout my shame and embarrassment, Lord, help me to heal. I must not be afraid of what other people think—or even what I think of myself. I know that You know all and see all, and yet You love me. Forgive me, Lord, and help me to forgive the others who have hurt me. I humbly bow before You and ask for Your healing.

Freedom from Fear

You did not receive a spirit that makes you a slave again to
fear, but you received the Spirit of sonship.
And by him we cry, "Abba, Father."
ROMANS 8:15

*L*ord, I ask in the name of Jesus that You would deliver me from fear. Let doubt be gone! Let cynicism flee! Instead of a spirit that makes me a slave again to fear, I have received the Spirit of sonship—or daughtership in my case. Abba, Father, rescue me from terror, dread, and the fearful anticipation of things that scare me. I cannot do this on my own. Deliver me, Lord, to Your freedom and peace.

Calm My Anxiety

When anxiety was great within me, your
consolation brought joy to my soul.

PSALM 94:19

*L*ord, I can feel anxiety rising inside like the mercury of a thermometer in July. Calm my nervousness and worry. Console me with Your truth that drives away restlessness and brings peace that we cannot comprehend. It's not because of anything I do, for I can't make the stress go away. By Your power, Lord, bring joy to my soul again—and let me be at peace.

God Is Your Comfort

He restores my soul. He guides me in paths of righteousness for his name's sake. Even
though I walk through the valley of the shadow of death, I will fear no evil, for you are
with me; your rod and your staff, they comfort me.

PSALM 23:3–4

*L*ord, there is none like You. When I am sad, You are my comfort. Your calm presence restores my soul. Your words are cool, refreshing water to my spirit. Despite my confusion, You guide me in paths of righteousness, and it's all for Your glory. Even when I feel like I'm lost in a dark valley, I will not be afraid—for You are with me. Your gentle strength and Your divine authority comfort me.

My Work

The Power of Influence

To this end I labor,
struggling with all his energy,
which so powerfully works in me.
COLOSSIANS 1:29

*T*here's no single face of today's working woman. Laurie homeschools most of her seven children. Cindy is a stay-at-home mom who telecommutes part-time to her downtown office, while Nancy travels to a different city most weeks for her corporate job. Judy, a single woman, works as a hospital chaplain, and Anne quit her job a year ago to care for her eighty-two-year-old father.

Whether our work takes us around the block or across the nation, we can become women of influence by becoming women of prayer. "Influence isn't about power and getting what we want," says Judith Couchman in *Designing a Woman's Life*. "It's about servanthood and giving our best to others, whatever our position in life."[10] Powerful, effective prayers make a difference as we partner with God to accomplish His work. With a servant's heart, we can build relational bridges and be a witness to God's love and saving power to those with whom we interact.

Whatever our station in life, we can pray powerfully as we intercede persistently for others. We need to keep at it, as we would our work. "A lack of endurance is one of the greatest causes of defeat, especially in prayer," writes Dutch Sheets in *Intercessory Prayer.* "We don't wait well. We're into microwaving; God, on the other hand, is usually into marinating."[11]

Prayer as a priority will help us juggle the multiple, often conflicting, duties of work, home, husband, children, friends, ministry, and, yes, even ourselves. In *Space for God*, Dan Postema says, "I used to write in my daily calendar '7–7:30 a.m.—Prayer.' But many times I passed that up. It was one more thing to pass by that day. Now I write '7–7:30 a.m.—God.' Somehow that's a little harder to neglect."[12]

When we pray, asking God to center us on Him and His good purposes, we'll find the balance we need in our work and life. We can ask for guidance and energy in determining priorities. We can lift up requests for a positive and helpful attitude at work and intercede for coworkers in conflict. We can pray for the ability and desire to serve with excellence, whether we work in the home or offsite. And we can thank God for the jobs we have—for the ability to shape and influence lives, whether they're our children's, our colleagues', or our clients'.

Thank You for My Work

It is good to praise the LORD and make
music to your name, O Most High.
PSALM 92:1

*L*ord, I praise You and thank You for my work. You are full of goodness and grace. My occupation gives me the ability to shape lives and influence people in positive ways every day, whether it's taking time for teachable moments with my kids or being a listening ear for a coworker. Thank You for my job and the ability to be a "missionary" wherever my feet tread. Season my words so that others may taste and see that my Lord is good.

God's Will for My Work Life

"For I know the plans I have for you," declares the LORD, "plans
to prosper you and not to harm you, plans to give you hope and a future."
JEREMIAH 29:11

*L*ord, I need wisdom and guidance in my work life. Please show me if this is the vocation I should be in right now or if I should change and find another job. I want to use my skills and abilities, as well as my interests, for Your glory. When I feel underutilized and yearn for something more, reveal to me where I can best serve in the coming season of my life.

Reaching Out to Others

The mouth of the righteous is a fountain of life.
PROVERBS 10:11

*L*ord, I want to be a woman of influence. I know that it's not about power or making myself look better—it's about giving to and assisting others. Help me be a witness to Your good things in my life. Teach me how to make a difference in my workplace each day—even with a kind word or a smile to someone who needs it. Provide opportunities to share Your love and help me know just what to say when the time comes.

Working with Excellence

Commit to the LORD whatever you do, and your plans will succeed.
PROVERBS 16:3

*L*ord, You give me work to do every day. Whether it's at home or in the marketplace, help me to honor You in my efforts. I don't want to be satisfied with mediocrity. I ask that You would empower me to do superior work and bring glory to Your name. Help me not to be a clock-watcher or time waster, but to find fulfillment in the tasks before me. Help me to be a woman of excellence, integrity, and good ideas in my place of employment.

Getting Along with Coworkers

*How good and pleasant it is
when brothers live together in unity!*
PSALM 133:1

*L*ord, I thank You for the people with whom I work and spend time every day. Help us to nurture an environment of peace and harmony. When people get along, it's a good thing! Give us respect for each other and patience to deal with disagreements. Even though we're all busy, help us to have more connectedness and unity so we can be more efficient and find more enjoyment in our work. Lord, please bless me and my relationships in the workplace.

Responding Well to Criticism

A fool shows his annoyance at once, but a prudent man overlooks an insult.
A truthful witness gives honest testimony, but a false witness tells lies.
Reckless words pierce like a sword, but the tongue of the wise brings healing.
PROVERBS 12:16–18

*L*ord, I don't like being criticized. I ask for a calm spirit when others make cutting remarks. Please give me insight to know if what is said is true—and if I need to make changes in my life. If not, Lord, I ask You to heal my heart from these verbal barbs. Please give me patience and discernment to keep my cool and not lash out in retaliation. Please bring our relationship through this criticism.

Blessings from the Work of Your Hands

The LORD your God will bless you in all your harvest
and in all the work of your hands, and your joy will be complete.
DEUTERONOMY 16:15

*L*ord, I ask that You would bless the work of my hands. As I sit at a computer or fold laundry or teach a classroom of children, may my work be meaningful and bear good fruit. I pray for a spirit of joy during the day as I go about my business. I pray for a cheerful countenance and a willing, servant's heart. I dedicate my work life to You, Lord, for Your good purposes and blessings.

Reducing Stress

Do not be anxious about anything, but in everything,
by prayer and petition, with thanksgiving, present your requests to God.
PHILIPPIANS 4:6

*L*ord, I have so much to do—please help me! Deadlines and details swirl around me like a swarm of bees. I feel intense pressure with my heavy workload. Help me to do what needs to be done each day so I can stop worrying and rest well at night. I give You my anxiety and stress—I release it all to You, Lord. As Your peace covers me, the peace that passes all understanding, may it guard my heart and mind in Christ Jesus. I rest in the comfort of Your love.

Balancing Work and Life

Am I now trying to win the approval of men, or of God? Or am I trying to please
men? If I were still trying to please men, I would not be a servant of Christ.
GALATIANS 1:10

*L*ord, every day is a juggling act with work, my home, my husband, kids, ministry, and friends. I rarely have time for myself—just to be with You, or even to remember who I am. Teach me to center on You, Lord, and keep my focus. I can't please everyone, and really, You've never asked me to. You are the One I seek to please. Be the hub of my heart, the steady center that moves the wheel of my life forward.

Servant Style Leadership

"Not so with you. Instead, whoever wants to become great among you must be your servant, and whoever wants to be first must be your slave—just as the Son of Man did not come to be served, but to serve, and to give his life as a ransom for many."

MATTHEW 20:26–28

*L*ord, teach me to be a leader by being a servant. Your ways are so unlike the ways of the world. Strange as it may seem, You say that "whoever wants to become great among you must be your servant." Help me to be more like Christ, as He did not come to be served, but to serve. Remove pride, selfishness, and arrogance from my life—and supply me, Lord, with humility and a heart that serves.

The Value of Motherhood

The wise woman builds her house, but with her own hands the foolish one tears hers down.

PROVERBS 14:1

*L*ord, I thank You that You value the calling of motherhood. As I work to serve my family and build our house into a home, I pray for wisdom, endurance, energy, and joy. Help me to know that raising children is a significant and high honor. I don't have to be in an office to be significant. Thank You for the privilege of building strong and lasting values into my children.

A Good Attitude

*"I have told you these things, so that in me you may have peace.
In this world you will have trouble. But take heart!
I have overcome the world."*
JOHN 16:33

*L*ord, I lift up to You my attitude at work. As I go about my day, may I have a positive outlook and a helpful spirit. Help me to be encouraging and supportive to others. Amid the activity—and sometimes the chaos—may my heart be at peace as the Holy Spirit strengthens and empowers me. Be the Lord of my emotions as I seek to serve You in my vocation.

Be Content

*I am not saying this because I am in need, for I have learned to
be content whatever the circumstances. I know what it is to
be in need, and I know what it is to have plenty. I have learned
the secret of being content in any and every situation, whether
well fed or hungry, whether living in plenty or in want.*

PHILIPPIANS 4:11–12

*L*ord, I often think about what could be and dream of a
better future. Sometimes, though, my thoughts are locked in
the past, stuck in disappointment and regret. Please help me
to be content with today, to live in this moment, no matter
what my current circumstances. In every situation, may I
look to You for peace. Still the storms in my heart so that
whether I am at rest or in motion, I can find your serenity
and strength.

Who's the Boss?

*In God I trust; I will not be afraid. What can man do to me?
I am under vows to you, O God; I will present my thank offerings to you.*

PSALM 56:11–12

*L*ord, I pray for a right mind-set with the person for whom
I work. Help me to submit to her authority and work with
honesty and integrity. Yet, while I report to someone in my
occupation, may I have the firm conviction that You are my
highest authority. My ultimate trust is in You, Lord, not in
any man or woman. As I report to You each day for guidance,
help me to serve You well.

The Power of Wise Stewardship

*His divine power has given us everything we need
for life and godliness through our knowledge of him
who called us by his own glory and goodness.*

2 PETER 1:3

*D*iane loves to shop. She jokes that she was born with a credit card in her hand—and she uses it freely at the mall. Her husband, Ben, is just the opposite. He won't buy anything unless it's on sale, and he painstakingly accounts for every penny he spends. Ben and Diane love God and each other, but they fight constantly over money issues.

Whether we are married, single, widowed, or divorced, whether we're a tightwad or a spendthrift, each of us has a need to pray powerfully for financial wisdom. If God is able to mend our broken bones and shattered hearts—and He is—He's also capable of fixing our finances.

God's Word has much to teach us about money and finance—in fact, there are well over two thousand verses in the Bible that refer to the topic of money. Clearly, our handling of money—our stewardship—is important to God and requires us to persevere in our prayer lives. God always answers our prayers. Sometimes He does so in ways that are quite unexpected.

When Sue was accepted to graduate school, she began to doubt whether she could really afford it. Sue prayed, saying, "God, if this is really what You want for me, then I need a sign. I think I need five thousand dollars." A few days later she received a check in the mail for exactly that amount. It was from her grandfather, who said he felt strongly led to send her money, in that amount, in that particular week. Now, whenever doubts arise in other areas of her life, Sue remembers God's faithfulness through this blessing.

God allows some to receive help and others to give it. Lydia was a wealthy woman whom God used for His good purposes. A "seller of purple" in Philippi, she heard the apostle Paul's message of Jesus Christ and responded. Lydia and her household were baptized, and she generously opened her home to Paul and his companions (Acts 16:14–15).

As we read key verses on financial topics, we become well equipped to pray targeted prayers that will help us control our spending, save for the future, get out of debt, and find contentment and balance. The power of prayer makes us generous givers and changes our attitude toward things. As we spend time praising God, we worry less and trust God more.

Biblical Perspective on Money

*Now it is required that those who have
been given a trust must prove faithful.*
1 CORINTHIANS 4:2

*L*ord, I am thankful for the financial resources with which You have blessed me. I want to be a good steward, a wise manager, of the resources You have entrusted to me. Help me to save and spend with discernment and to give to others in need. Help me to find balance—not be a hoarder or an out-of-control spender. Give me a godly view of money and how to use it in ways that will honor You.

Spending Wisely

*For the love of money is a root of all kinds of evil. Some people,
eager for money, have wandered from the faith and
pierced themselves with many griefs.*
1 TIMOTHY 6:10

*L*ord, You are the One who gives wisdom—and I ask that you would give me the discernment I need to spend money sensibly. I need money to pay my bills and meet my obligations. I know from Your Word that money itself is not evil; it's the love of money—greed—that makes us wander from the faith. Help me to spend the money You provide not in self-indulgence but in good judgment.

Saving and Investing

In the house of the wise are stores of choice food and oil,
but a foolish man devours all he has.
PROVERBS 21:20

*L*ord, I pray that You would lead me to wise financial advice. When I look, help me to find a trusted source who can give me direction as to where to best save and invest my resources. Please provide for my needs today and help me to save for the future. Help me to be responsible with my finances as I trust You as my provider.

Joy in Giving

Each man should give what he has decided in his heart to give,
not reluctantly or under compulsion, for God loves a cheerful giver.
2 CORINTHIANS 9:7

*L*ord, I thank You for Your blessings. Whether in plenty or with little, I want to be a cheerful giver. I desire to give from a full heart that serves, not reluctantly or with complaining. I long to see Your money used in ways that will bless others—through my tithing at church, giving to mission organizations, or helping the needy. I choose to give at whatever level I can—and ask You to bless it.

Honesty and Trust

An honest answer is like a kiss on the lips.
PROVERBS 24:26

*L*ord, help me to be honest as I communicate about my finances—my salary, my savings, my debt, my loans, and my taxes—with the man I share my life with. In all our dealings with money, help us to have integrity. Lord, honor our desire to be truthful and reliable in our words and actions with each other. Empower us to be people who keep our word, people who are upright in all of our financial matters.

Better Communication about Finances

Wives, submit to your husbands, as is fitting in the Lord. Husbands, love your wives and do not be harsh with them.
COLOSSIANS 3:18–19

*L*ord, I am tired of arguing about money. Please give my husband and me the ability to communicate better in this area of our lives. Help us to speak with integrity and listen with respect and understanding. Help us to make our words kind, not harsh, as we seek to prioritize and find order in our finances. Even when we don't agree, help us to see the other person's point of view and find ways to resolve our conflicts.

Dealing with Debt

I call on the LORD in my distress, and he answers me.
PSALM 120:1

*L*ord, I need help. My debt is mounting higher and higher; it's getting out of control. Please show me creative ways to pay it off, and help me to save and spend with wisdom. I ask for the resources to pay down my credit cards, loans, and other debts. Show me where I can cut back on spending so I'll have more funds available. Lord, please clean up this mess I've created. Reveal to me the ways I can learn from this and begin again.

Help for a Materialistic Attitude

Keep your lives free from the love of money and be content with what you have,
because God has said, "Never will I leave you; never will I forsake you."
HEBREWS 13:5

*L*ord, at times I'm so affected by this world—I am tempted to want what others have or long for things that I see on television. Change my attitude, Lord. Help me to understand that acquiring more "stuff" won't necessarily make me happy. Being filled with *You* brings true contentment. Teach me the joy and lasting satisfaction that comes from looking solely to You, Lord.

God Will Provide

"Therefore I tell you, do not worry about your life, what you
will eat or drink; or about your body, what you will wear.
Is not life more important than food, and the body more
important than clothes? Look at the birds of the air; they
do not sow or reap or store away in barns, and yet your heavenly
Father feeds them. Are you not much more valuable than they?
Who of you by worrying can add a single hour to his life?"
MATTHEW 6:25–27

*L*ord, I thank You for providing for my needs. I give You my worries and fears—those nagging thoughts about lacking money for clothes, food, and the basics of life. You feed the sparrows in the field, Lord—You'll certainly help me and my family. Your resources are limitless—You have an abundance of blessings. I praise You for Your goodness, Lord, and the faithfulness of Your provision.

Teaching Our Kids about Money

Do not be deceived: God cannot be mocked. A man reaps what he sows.
GALATIANS 6:7

*L*ord, I ask for Your insight as I teach my children about the wise use of money. Help me to impress upon them the importance of saving, tithing, and giving as well as spending in balanced ways. Your Word reveals the principle of "sowing and reaping." As I teach my kids how to surrender their financial lives to You, please bless the work of our hands—like a gardener who sows seeds and reaps a harvest of beautiful blossoms.

God's Healing in My Financial Matters

"I have seen his ways, but I will heal him; I will
guide him and restore comfort to him."
ISAIAH 57:18

*L*ord, I ask for healing in my financial life. I have not always done right, and circumstances have put me behind—but I want things to be better. I ask that You would restore my marriage relationship as my husband and I seek to work through our conflicts over money. I ask that You would guide me in the wise use of my resources and replenish what I have lost. I want to honor You, Lord, and be a blessing to others.

What Is Success?

*Command them to do good, to be rich in good deeds,
and to be generous and willing to share.*
1 TIMOTHY 6:18

*L*ord, when I think of "living well," help me to be drawn toward *Your* ways, not the world's. Show me the difference between what I *want* and what I really *need*. Help me to know that my true success lies in being rich in love, wealthy in good works toward others, and generous in sharing from Your abundant blessing. I thank You for the prosperity You provide, inside and out.

Treasures in Heaven

*"Do not store up for yourselves treasures on earth, where moth
and rust destroy, and where thieves break in and steal. But store
up for yourselves treasures in heaven, where moth and rust
do not destroy, and where thieves do not break in and steal.
For where your treasure is, there your heart will be also."*
MATTHEW 6:19–21

*L*ord, You are my true treasure. I value all that You are—
holy, wise, loving, and just. You are mighty and powerful, the
giver of life. Help me to take my eyes off *things* as a source of
meaning; they may be nice and helpful, but inevitably they
fade away. My hope is in You, Lord, and my fortune to come,
in heaven.

Prayer for a Married Couple's Finances

*"No one can serve two masters. Either he will hate the one
and love the other, or he will be devoted to the one and despise the other.
You cannot serve both God and Money."*
MATTHEW 6:24

*L*ord, we ask You for wisdom and harmony in our financial
life. We choose to serve You, God. Forgive us when we
have been selfish, when we've gone to extremes of spending
or hoarding. Heal us when we need restoration in our
finances. Help us not to argue, but to learn better ways to
communicate—to be honest and to seek to understand the
other person's perspective even when we may not agree. We
thank You for the ways You have provided and for Your
amazing answers to prayer!

My Church

The Power of Worship

Help me, Lord, to remember that religion
is not to be confined to the church...
nor exercised only in prayer and meditation,
but that everywhere I am in Thy Presence.
SUSANNA WESLEY (MOTHER OF JOHN WESLEY)

*P*owerful prayer is essential to building and growing a healthy church. Much more than just a building, the church is a place to belong and feel welcome. It's a family of believers, brothers and sisters in the Lord, who, imperfect as they are, seek to love, forgive, connect, and serve together. It's a place to find God's truth, healing, and wholeness as we read the Bible and seek to apply it to our lives.

The church is also a place of service. When we discover and use our spiritual gifts, we build up the body of Christ, those people within, and seek to fulfill the Great Commission by reaching outside to those in need.

Most important, God's house is a place of prayer (Isaiah 56:7) and worship (John 4:24). It is through these two essentials—prayer and worship—that we can see revival in our own lives and, we hope, in the ends of the earth.

The power of God is released as we worship with other believers. "This kind of *corporate* praise can pull you in and take you someplace you couldn't get to without it. There is something that happens when we worship God together with other believers that doesn't happen to the same degree when we don't. It becomes a force that ignites change in the world around you. There's a renewing, reviving, and refreshing of our own souls," says Stormie Omartian in *The Prayer That Changes Everything.*[13] God releases His blessings through worship.

If you're not sure how to lift up prayers of praise, try this: Acknowledge God's presence and speak His wonderful qualities. Tell Him of His greatness—*You are holy, You are worthy, You are righteous. Power and majesty belong to You, O Lord. Thank you for your mercy, love, patience, goodness, and grace. I praise You, Lord.*

It doesn't matter if we're beginners or experienced prayer warriors. Our prayers don't have to be perfect. God considers the attitude of the heart. When your intention is to honor Him, He is pleased. Just as a caring mom enjoys the scribbles of her five-year-old and displays them proudly on her refrigerator, our attempts at praising God become His works of art.

Thank You for My Church Family

Therefore, as we have opportunity, let us do good
to all people, especially to those who belong to the family of believers.
GALATIANS 6:10

*L*ord, I thank You for my church and the people there, my brothers and sisters in Christ. May we grow together as a "family" of believers as we learn to love and serve each other. Although we are different, help us to respect each other and seek to build up one another. It is a blessing to have people to experience life with, both the good times and the bad. May we be better connected as we all learn to know You and love You more.

Prayer for Pastor and His Family

We always thank God, the Father of our Lord Jesus Christ,
when we pray for you, because we have heard of your faith
in Christ Jesus and of the love you have for all the saints.
COLOSSIANS 1:3–4

*L*ord, I thank You for our pastor. He is a blessing to our church. I pray that You would enable him with strong leadership skills and wise decision-making abilities. Help him to be a godly man, devoted to seeking and following You. Protect him and his family from the temptations of the world. Though he may have a heavy load, please be His continual refreshment. Help him to guard his time with his family, and keep them strong and loving.

Prayer for a Church's Staff

*On the contrary, we speak as men approved by God
to be entrusted with the gospel. We are not trying to
please men but God, who tests our hearts.*
1 THESSALONIANS 2:4

*L*ord, I thank You for all the committed people who work on staff at our church. Thank You for their faithful service every day in the offices and on committees. Help them in their daily decisions to serve You and not to seek to please people. May they do their jobs efficiently and well so that all they do builds up the church and furthers Your kingdom.

Prayer for Sunday School, Bible Study, and Small Group Leaders

*The body is a unit, though it is made up of many parts; and
though all its parts are many, they form one body. So it is with Christ.
For we were all baptized by one Spirit into one body—whether
Jews or Greeks, slave or free—and we were all given the one Spirit to drink.*
1 CORINTHIANS 12:12–13

*L*ord, I thank You for the faithful servants who teach in our Sunday school, Bible studies, and small groups. Week after week they present the truth from Your Word to help children and adults know You better. Though we all have different functions in the church, we are all one body—and I thank You that You knit us all together in unity. Bless these men and women who serve for Your glory.

Prayer for Church Service Ministries and Volunteers

Therefore I glory in Christ Jesus in my service to God.
ROMANS 15:17

*L*ord, I praise You that You raise up people to serve the needs of our church. Bless the ones who provide for us as worship leaders, ushers, greeters, sound and media workers, and the entire church ministry team. Bless the kitchen workers, nursery workers, parking lot attendants, ushers, maintenance staff, and others—all the people in front or behind the scenes, Lord, who keep our church running smoothly and well.

Prayer for Revival

"But you will receive power when the Holy Spirit
comes on you; and you will be my witnesses in Jerusalem,
and in all Judea and Samaria, and to the ends of the earth."
ACTS 1:8

*L*ord, we pray for the Holy Spirit's power to come in a mighty way to each individual who attends our church. As we find personal revival, may it grow to light a mighty fire of passion for God in our church—then spread to our community, our nation, and our world. Please give us a heart to pray for revival and hands that put our faith to action with service to others.

Prayer for Missionaries

Then Jesus came to them and said, "All authority in heaven and
on earth has been given to me. Therefore go and make disciples of
all nations, baptizing them in the name of the Father and of the Son and of the Holy
Spirit, and teaching them to obey everything I have commanded you.
And surely I am with you always, to the very end of the age."
MATTHEW 28:18–20

*L*ord, I thank You for our missionaries, both foreign and domestic. Empower them, fill them, and sustain them as they seek to fulfill Your great commission. Give them godly wisdom and good communication as they preach, teach, disciple, and baptize people from all nations. Please meet their needs for a close relationship with You, give them protection and safety, and provide for their financial needs. And, Lord, bless them with emotionally healthy relationships and harmony on their team.

Prayer for Good Relationships

"My command is this: Love each other as I have loved you."
JOHN 15:12

*L*ord, I pray for each member of this church—that we would get along. Despite our variety of backgrounds and opinions, help us to live and worship in harmony. Give us the ability to value and respect our differences. Protect us against divisions, and help us to be like-minded. We all have different gifts, roles, and functions, but we are collectively one body, Lord—Yours. Bind us together with ties of faith and fruitfulness.

Prayer for Welcoming Newcomers

Welcome him in the Lord with great joy.
PHILIPPIANS 2:29

*L*ord, I pray that we would be a welcoming church for members, guests, and newcomers alike. Help us to receive new people with warmth and love. Give us sensitive hearts to notice others—we don't want to focus only on our own family or group of friends. We were all once "the new person," so help us to be inclusive and make visitors feel at home in our church.

Prayer for Solid Teaching from God's Word

"Watch out for false prophets. They come to you in sheep's clothing, but inwardly they are ferocious wolves. By their fruit you will recognize them. Do people pick grapes from thornbushes, or figs from thistles? Likewise every good tree bears good fruit, but a bad tree bears bad fruit. A good tree cannot bear bad fruit, and a bad tree cannot bear good fruit. Every tree that does not bear good fruit is cut down and thrown into the fire. Thus, by their fruit you will recognize them."

MATTHEW 7:15–20

*L*ord, I pray that the Word of God would be taught at our church in a faithful and honest way. I pray against false teaching or doctrines that are deceptive. Help us to grow in godliness because we have the truth taught and preached with integrity. Nurture our souls with solid teaching so we can be equipped to serve others—to be salt and light in a dark world, a world that needs Your love, power, and peace.

Encouraging One Another

Let us not give up meeting together, as some are in the habit of doing, but let us encourage one another—and all the more as you see the Day approaching.

HEBREWS 10:25

*L*ord, I thank You for my church and the people who attend. Whether I know them all or not, help me to be a blessing to each person I meet. Help me to be an encourager, a listener. May we build each other up, not tear each other down. May we be others-centered and see the value of each person in our congregation. Lord, help us to be a blessing to them in any way we can.

Worshiping Together

*"God is spirit, and his worshipers must
worship in spirit and in truth."*
JOHN 4:24

*L*ord, we want to worship You! We praise Your
holy name and ask that You would bless us as we
worship You in spirit and in truth. As we join
together, let the musicians, choir, and leaders guide
us in a chorus of resounding praise and adoration.
You are worthy and wonderful, Lord. Thank You
for all You are and all You do for us. I praise You
and I bless You, Lord.

Prayer

"These I will bring to my holy mountain and give them joy in my house of prayer.
Their burnt offerings and sacrifices will be accepted on my altar; for
my house will be called a house of prayer for all nations."

ISAIAH 56:7

*L*ord, Your house is a house of prayer for all nations. Thank You for the gift of prayer, our two-way conversation with You. Help us to make prayer a priority every day. Lead us as we lift up our adoration, confession, thanksgiving, and supplication—of asking You for everything we need. May we be intercessors, praying for other people and their needs. May we bask in the glory of Your light so we can reflect the Father's heart to all we meet. Lord, teach us to pray.

Spiritual Gifts

Just as each of us has one body with many members,
and these members do not all have the same function. . .

ROMANS 12:4

*L*ord, help us to discover and use our spiritual gifts, those talents and abilities You've given us to serve You in the church and in outreach ministries. We are many, but we form one body. We have different gifts, according to what You've graciously given, but we serve each other. If our gift is prophesying, let us do so in proportion to our faith. If it is serving, let us do that joyfully. If it is teaching, let us teach; if it is encouraging, let us build others up; if it is contributing to needs, let us give generously; if it is leadership, let us govern diligently; if it is showing mercy, let us do it cheerfully. Whatever other gifts we have, may we use them for Your glory, too.

The Power of Reaching Out

Whatever you do, work at it with all your heart,
as working for the Lord, not for men.
COLOSSIANS 3:23

*M*inistry is for every woman. It's not just a "calling" for pastors, missionaries, and evangelists.

Maribeth's ministry is in music; she sings and worships by playing her flute at church. Kim heads a worship dance ministry and blesses women in prisons with a moving presentation of the gospel. Donna teaches Sunday school and pours her joyful spirit into energetic three-year-olds every week.

Many years ago, God chose a woman named Miriam to be a prophetess and worship leader, helping her brothers Moses and Aaron in bringing the people of Israel out of their slavery in Egypt. God miraculously allowed the people to walk through the Red Sea on dry ground—and then caused the waters to wash away the pursuing Egyptian army (Exodus 14–15). After the safe crossing, Miriam led worship, "and all the women followed her, with tambourines and dancing. Miriam sang to them: 'Sing to the LORD, for he is highly exalted. The horse and its rider he has hurled into the sea'" (Exodus 15:20–21).

Whether God uses us for His service in the church, a Christian organization, or on the mission field, our ministry needs to be covered in prayer. As we reach up to God, He fills us so we can reach out—and pour His love and blessing into others.

Effective ministry is not based on our abilities. We don't make it happen ourselves—we partner with God through prayer, and He provides the power. As we ask in faith, and go about our Father's business, the Holy Spirit brings deliverance and acts according to God's will for the answer.

One of the best ways we can minister to others is by praying for them. It's not always easy, but it's always worth it. "In real prayer, we go places we don't want to go," says Patricia Raybon in *I Told the Mountain to Move.* "We learn lessons we don't want to learn. We tell secrets we don't want to tell. We walk bridges we don't want to cross. We face battles we don't want to fight. Then we change the world. We stand at the door to heaven and then we rush in."[14]

When we pray for our ministry, we can ask God to give us the willingness and compassion to serve others. If we are not sure where to spend our time, we can ask God to help us identify our spiritual gifts and to use them effectively. When we are tired, we can ask the Holy Spirit for energy and refreshment, along with the discernment to balance work, home, and rest with our ministry opportunities. We can also ask God to help our ministry grow, and provide the resources (financial and otherwise) to implement new ideas.

Praising God pleases Him, too. He is the One who empowers us to serve faithfully and be effective.

Release More Power in My Ministry

*May the God of peace, who through the blood of the eternal
covenant brought back from the dead our Lord Jesus,
that great Shepherd of the sheep, equip you with everything
good for doing his will, and may he work in us what is
pleasing to him, through Jesus Christ, to whom be glory
for ever and ever. Amen.*
HEBREWS 13:20–21

*L*ord God, I need You. I ask that You would release more of Your power into my life and ministry. God of peace, equip me with everything good to do Your will. Help me to have compassion, integrity, and wise leadership. Work in me what is pleasing to You, Lord. Empower me, enlighten me, and change me so I can be more effective in serving. Let Your name be glorified and honored in all of my ministry activities.

Wisdom and Understanding

*Blessed is the man who finds wisdom,
the man who gains understanding,*
PROVERBS 3:13

*L*ord, I pray for insight into the people I serve. Give me understanding as to their needs so I can better relate to them and be able to address their concerns. Help me to take an interest in their particular culture, whether ethnic or age-related. I pray for wisdom on how to reach them, teach them, and bless them.

A Heart to Serve

*The LORD is gracious and compassionate,
slow to anger and rich in love.*
PSALM 145:8

*L*ord, I pray for a spirit of compassion. Help me to care about the needs of others and have genuine love for the ones I serve. Pour into me Your caring, kind spirit, so I can be a blessing and minister out of a full heart. Fill me to overflowing so my ministry will be effective, growing, and blessed. May I walk in Your graciousness with a heart to serve.

Protection and Safety

*The LORD will protect him and preserve his life;
he will bless him in the land and not surrender
him to the desire of his foes.*
PSALM 41:2

*L*ord, You are my strength—please protect me. You are my safety—preserve me. Keep me safe in Your tender care as I minister to the needs of others. And please protect those around me, the ones to whom I minister. Bless me, Lord, and keep me from my enemies—the ones I see and the ones I don't. I ask for a strong wall of protection to keep out evil and keep in good. I trust You, My strong and mighty Lord.

Managing Stress

. . .and his incomparably great power for us who believe. That power is like the working of his mighty strength, which he exerted in Christ when he raised him from the dead and seated him at his right hand in the heavenly realms, far above all rule and authority, power and dominion, and every title that can be given, not only in the present age but also in the One to come.
EPHESIANS 1:19–21

*L*ord, I am tired. I have been doing too much, and I need rest. Please help me to manage my priorities—my home life, work, ministry, and rest—in better ways so I have more balance and less stress. I don't want to get burned out. I want to be effective for You. I pray that the same power that raised Jesus Christ from the dead, the "incomparably great power for us who believe," would awaken my worn-out body and spirit. Replenish me and restore me for Your glory.

Provision and Resources

The next day we landed at Sidon; and Julius, in kindness to Paul,
allowed him to go to his friends so they might provide for his needs.
ACTS 27:3

*L*ord, Your resources are unlimited. You delight to give Your children good gifts, to meet their needs. I boldly and humbly ask that You would provide for the needs of my ministry. Bring our ministry to the minds of people who are willing to give out of their God-given resources. May they give of their time, money, talents, or other resources to bless these ministry efforts to further Your kingdom.

Leadership

. . .if it is encouraging, let him encourage; if it is contributing to
the needs of others, let him give generously; if it is leadership, let
him govern diligently; if it is showing mercy, let him do it cheerfully.
ROMANS 12:8

*L*ord, teach me Your ways. Show me how to be a leader who is first a servant. You showed us servant leadership when You washed the feet of Your disciples. Humble, I come, Lord—let me be more like You. Deal with my pride and sin and selfishness, and help me to serve others with the right motives. Help me to be diligent in my tasks and encouraging in my words. Let me lead, Lord, with love.

Raise Up Volunteers

When he saw the crowds, he had compassion on them, because
they were harassed and helpless, like sheep without a shepherd. Then
he said to his disciples, "The harvest is plentiful but the workers are few.
Ask the Lord of the harvest, therefore, to send out workers into his harvest field."
MATTHEW 9:36–38

*L*ord, the world is our mission field. From the nursery at church to the orphanages across the sea, there are children who need love and attention. From the streets of Columbus to the slums of Calcutta, people need to hear the Good News. The harvest is plentiful and the workers are few—but I ask You, Lord of the harvest, to bring out people with hearts to serve. May they help my ministry and others in our nation and around the world.

For the Poor and Needy

"When you give to the needy, do not let your left hand know what
your right hand is doing, so that your giving may be in secret.
Then your Father, who sees what is done in secret, will reward you."
MATTHEW 6:3–4

*L*ord, I pray today for the poor and needy. Many need money, while others are poor in spirit. Please provide food and water to meet their physical needs and the gospel of Jesus Christ and His saving love to fill their souls. Lord, show me how I can be part of the solution. Show me where I can give and serve. Use my abilities and finances to help, for Your glory.

For Those in Prison

"I was in prison and you came to visit me."
MATTHEW 25:36

*L*ord, I pray for the men and women in prison all over our country today. I ask for a revival—that many would come to know You, love You, and serve You. Help those who are incarcerated to know that You are the One who sets people free from the bondage of sin and wrongdoing. Help them to know that only You offer a life of hope and peace. In the darkness, help them to find Christ's forgiveness, joy, and light. Remind my heart, Lord, to visit those in prison and fulfill Your commands.

For the Sick

Is any one of you sick? He should call the elders of the church to pray over him and anoint him with oil in the name of the Lord. And the prayer offered in faith will make the sick person well; the Lord will raise him up. If he has sinned, he will be forgiven. Therefore confess your sins to each other and pray for each other so that you may be healed. The prayer of a righteous man is powerful and effective.
JAMES 5:14–16

*L*ord, I am praying for a person who is sick right now. She needs your healing touch on her body and her emotions. Heal her pain, Lord. Help her to sense Your presence, to know You are near. Be her comfort. I ask that she would not be afraid or lonely. I pray in faith, in the name and power of Jesus, to heal my friend. I ask that You would make her well.

For Those in Grief

"Blessed are those who mourn, for they will be comforted."
MATTHEW 5:4

*L*ord, my friend has deep pain in her soul. I ask that You would comfort her. Be near, Lord, be near. May she rest in the strong and loving arms of the One who loves her most. Heal her heartache, heal her sorrow. You are acquainted with grief, so You know her pain. Help her to know that You can relate and that You care. One day soon, may she find healing and wholeness again.

Doing Greater Works

*"I tell you the truth, anyone who has faith in me will do
what I have been doing. He will do even greater things than these,
because I am going to the Father. And I will do whatever you
ask in my name, so that the Son may bring glory to the Father."*

JOHN 14:12–13

*L*ord, You are so amazing. You said we would do even greater things than You accomplished while on earth. I pray for great faith, that I may be a part of doing Your greater works. You healed the sick, made the lame walk, and radically changed Your generation. Empower me to help and heal in whatever way You call me to. May it delight You to answer my prayers and bring glory to Yourself.

Power of the Holy Spirit

*Our gospel came to you not simply with words, but also
with power, with the Holy Spirit and with deep conviction.*

1 THESSALONIANS 1:5

*L*ord, in my own human effort I cannot make this ministry happen. I am totally dependent on You. I ask and pray for the power of Your Holy Spirit to fill me and work through me. Jump-start the compassion and conviction in my heart to minister life to others. Recharge me in my spirit and body to serve You effectively and well.

My Friends

The Power of Connection

A friend loves at all times.
PROVERBS 17:17

*W*hat would we do without friends? They encourage and inspire us. They listen as if they really care—because they do. Good friends seek to understand and empathize with us. Even when they can't relate, they care about us anyway.

Friends are fun! We enjoy being around them. When we can talk, laugh, pray, and play with someone we trust, we have found a real treasure. We give and receive, we love and we learn. Above all, in friendship, we seek what is best for each other. No matter what our age or life stage, we never outgrow our need for connection, for having and being a good friend.

Loving with words and actions is a hallmark of true friendship. I remember once being stressed for weeks about an important deadline at work. The project weighed heavily on me, so I had been living on snacks instead of using my precious time to grocery shop. On top of it all, I was beginning to feel a sore throat coming on. When my friend Maria learned I was getting ill, she promptly came with four bags of groceries from the health food store—and prayed for me to stay well. I was astonished at her thoughtful generosity. And I soon began to feel better.

Like snowflakes, no two friendships are the same;

each brings a unique beauty and joy to our lives. We have acquaintances, casual friends, close friends, and "heart" friends, that handful of women with whom we share our deepest selves. Jesus had different circles of friends, too. He ministered to the crowds, He spent significant time with the twelve disciples, and He was closest to three men: Peter, James, and John. He was companion to tax collectors and sinners (Mark 2:15–17), as well as to His dearly loved friends Mary, Martha, and Lazarus (John 11:20–32).

Today each of us can have the joy of knowing Jesus as our friend (John 15:15). In the quiet solitude of prayer, we can pour out our deepest fears and desires. We can take pleasure in enjoying God—in just being in His company. "Fellowship with him [Jesus] is a matter of priorities and a matter of choice," says Ken Gire in *Intimate Moments with the Savior*. "It's the better part of the meal life has to offer. It is, in fact, the main course."[15]

When we fellowship with God in prayer, we can then pray powerfully for our earthly friends. We can pray *for* them and *with* them in Jesus' name.

That's perhaps one of the best ways we can show a friend we care. Maybe someone we know is going through a separation or divorce and could use a phone call. Perhaps a new neighbor, a recent widow, or a new mom may need the unexpected blessing of friendly kindness. Maybe we should stop to thank God for the wonderful women in our lives— those women who've given us the gift of friendship—and ask Him how we can be a better friend to others.

Thank You for My Friendships

*A man of many companions may come to ruin, but there
is a friend who sticks closer than a brother.*
PROVERBS 18:24

*L*ord, I thank You for my wonderful friends! As I think about the treasure chest of my close friends, casual friends, and acquaintances, I am grateful for the blessings and the joys each one brings to my life. Thank You for my "heart" friends, my loyal sister friends who listen, care, and encourage me. They are my faithful companions. I acknowledge that You, Lord, are the giver of all good gifts, and I thank You for Your provision in my friendships.

A Deeper Walk with God

*I keep asking that the God of our Lord Jesus Christ, the glorious Father, may give
you the Spirit of wisdom and revelation, so that you may know him better. I pray also
that the eyes of your heart may be enlightened in order that you may know the hope
to which he has called you, the riches of his glorious inheritance in the saints, and his
incomparably great power for us who believe.*
EPHESIANS 1:17–19

*L*ord, I ask in Jesus' name that my unsaved friend would come to know You as her personal Savior. I pray for her salvation and for her growth in faith. As You reveal Yourself to her, may she come to truly experience You—not just in her head, but in her heart. Draw her closer to You, Lord, so she may feel the power of Your presence. Revive her spirit, Lord, for her sake and Your glory.

Praying for My Friends' Needs

My intercessor is my friend as my eyes pour out tears to God
JOB 16:20

*L*ord, help me to have wisdom as I pray for the needs of my friends. I want to be an intercessor, to come before You as one who stands in the gap. Whether she is hurting or sick or needs direction, I am here asking You to help her and heal her. Give her courage and faith in her trials. May Your gracious hand be upon her life.

Friends Help Each Other

*If one falls down, his friend can help him up. But pity the
man who falls and has no one to help him up!*
ECCLESIASTES 4:10

*L*ord, sometimes it's easier to give than to receive. I want to be a giver, to take the time to care and help my friends when they need it. And help me to learn to receive, too—so that I'm not too proud to receive generosity from a friend. Give and take, Lord. . .we really do need each other.

Friends Love Each Other

*A friend loves at all times, and
a brother is born for adversity.*
PROVERBS 17:17

*L*ord, help me to be a friend who loves at all times, even when I may not feel like it. Teach me how to love with words—to be encouraging and supportive—and help me to show love by my actions, too. I want to be a better listener, never self-centered. Show me how to bring joy to others in tangible ways, with a phone call, a hug, or a deed that is meaningful to my friend.

Friends Forgive Each Other

When Jesus saw their faith, he said, "Friend, your sins are forgiven."
LUKE 5:20

*L*ord, I humbly ask that You would forgive me for any ways I have hurt my friend. Help me to deal with things I'm aware of, and bring to my mind the things I'm not. Please give me the courage and faith to forgive my friend when she hurts me, Lord. I know that all my wrongdoings are forgiven by You when I confess them. May I be a person who in turn forgives others.

Jesus Is Your Friend

"Greater love has no one than this, that he lay down his life for his friends. You are my friends if you do what I command. I no longer call you servants, because a servant does not know his master's business. Instead, I have called you friends, for everything that I learned from my Father I have made known to you."
JOHN 15:13–15

*L*ord, You are my best friend. How could it be anyone else! You are kind, loving, generous, faithful, and giving. You always listen, and You always care. And You have the best advice. But most of all, You laid down Your life for me—for *me*, Lord! There is no greater expression of love, and for that I am immensely grateful. Thank You for calling me Your friend. Help me to learn Your ways so I can be a better friend to others.

I Need Closer Friendships

Be devoted to one another in brotherly love.
Honor one another above yourselves.

ROMANS 12:10

*L*ord, I feel as if my friends are distant and busy. They don't seem to have time for me. Maybe I've been preoccupied, too. I ask that You would bring closer friendships into my life. I need to feel connected. I need their support and encouragement. Show me where I need to reach out more to others. Help me to listen, seek to understand, and offer unconditional love and acceptance—and find the same in return.

Dealing with Enemies

Do not repay anyone evil for evil. Be careful to do what is right in the eyes of
everybody. If it is possible, as far as it depends on you, live at peace with everyone.
Do not take revenge, my friends, but leave room for God's wrath, for it is written:
"It is mine to avenge; I will repay," says the Lord. On the contrary: "If your
enemy is hungry, feed him; if he is thirsty, give him something to drink. In doing
this, you will heap burning coals on his head." Do not be overcome by evil, but
overcome evil with good.

ROMANS 12:17–21

*L*ord, I need wisdom in dealing with my adversaries. Teach me Your ways of justice, and help me to do what is right. I will not repay anyone evil for evil. I will not take it into my own hands, but I will allow You to avenge. I ask that You would bring good results from the iniquity of this situation. Give me the grace to leave it to You to make things right again. Please grant me the strength to live in peace.

I Need More Friends

Turn to me and be gracious to me, for I am lonely and afflicted.
PSALM 25:16

*L*ord, I have been so lonely lately—I need more friends. In Your graciousness, please provide for my need for companionship. It's hard to start again, to find someone who cares and makes the time for a new person in her life. But You are the giver of good things, and I trust that You will bring the right people at the right time. As I seek to extend the hand of friendship to others, give me wisdom to know which relationships to pursue. Bless me with good friends, Lord.

Reaching Out to Others

"You have heard that it was said, 'Love your neighbor and hate your enemy.'"
MATTHEW 5:43

*L*ord, would You please show me how I can reach out to someone who needs a friend? Bring to mind people with whom I can share the love of Christ. Let my words and actions reflect Your love, acceptance, and compassion. Give me eyes to see the needs and a heart to respond. As I look out for the needs of others, and not just my own, I pray that I would be a vessel of Your blessing and joy.

When I Don't Know What to Pray

In the same way, the Spirit helps us in our weakness. We do not know what we ought to pray for, but the Spirit himself intercedes for us with groans that words cannot express. And he who searches our hearts knows the mind of the Spirit, because the Spirit intercedes for the saints in accordance with God's will.
ROMANS 8:26–27

*L*ord, You know my friend's needs and the desires of her heart. But sometimes I don't know what to say or how to pray. Holy Spirit, You are the One who helps us in our weakness. When I do not know what to pray for, You intercede for me with groans that words cannot express. Search my heart and intercede for my friend today, Lord. I pray that Your will would be done.

Restoring a Broken Friendship

Above all, love each other deeply, because
love covers over a multitude of sins.
1 PETER 4:8

*L*ord, I thank You for Your healing balm that covers the hurt and pain I've experienced in this friendship. Your grace covers me. Your love repairs my brokenness, and You give me the ability to love again. Help me to put aside the wounds of my heart and to be a friend again. I thank You and praise You that Your love is healing and restoring. Thank You, Lord, for putting this friendship back together.

Being a Better Listener

Come and listen, all you who fear God;
let me tell you what he has done for me.
PSALM 66:16

*L*ord, I praise You today for all You have done for me. You have brought help, hope, healing, and restoration, and I want to tell people! Help me proclaim Your goodness, sharing the amazing ways You have come through for me. But as I speak, help me to be a good listener, too. Through Your Spirit, Lord, may I show I care about my friends. Give me wisdom to know when my ears should be open and my mouth shut.

My Extended Family

The Power of Persistence

You don't choose your family.
They are God's gift to you,
as you are to them.
DESMOND TUTU

*T*he family tree in some people's lives is more like a forest. Their extended family includes grandparents, aunts, uncles, cousins, nieces, nephews, second cousins once removed (whatever that means). . .and on and on and on. In other families, there just aren't many relatives—and "family" ties are formed with nonrelated individuals, such as friends, neighbors, or fellow church members.

Whether your extended family is large or small, related or unrelated, you can bless these people in your lives by praying for them.

How can we pray powerfully for our extended family? As with any prayer, persistence is key. Persistent prayer is illustrated in a story Jesus told His disciples about a widow and a judge. The woman approached the judge, asking for justice against her enemy. The judge refused to help, but she kept pestering him, resolutely determined to get things right. Finally, the judge said to himself, "Even though I don't fear God or care about men, yet because this widow keeps bothering me, I will see that she gets justice, so that she won't eventually wear me out with her coming!" (Luke 18:4–5).

Like this woman, I pursued God persistently over a family member's salvation. Dom, my mother's second husband, was a self-proclaimed "educated" man who would have nothing to do with God. My siblings and I shared God's love and truth with him for twelve long years, even enduring his anger when we wanted to attend church services on Christmas Eve. I recall him once yelling, "Why do you kids have to go to church tonight? Christmas isn't about God, it's about family!" Actually, I thought to myself, Christmas *is* all about God.

Ultimately, Dom died of a terminal illness—but not before my mother had the privilege of hearing him ask Jesus Christ to be his Savior, just two days before he entered eternity. This stubborn old man is now in the presence of God forever, and his story reminds us never to give up. Trust God's timing, and pray on.

Whether we are close to our extended family or not, we can pray for them. As we thank God for our relatives, we can pray blessings on their lives. We can pray for their needs—even basic ones like wisdom and energy for daily living. We can pray for the generations to come, that they will know the Lord and serve Him. We can ask God to bless and protect those who are like family to us—our friends, neighbors, church family, and others.

Even when you don't know what to pray, ask God to bless your extended family, knowing that He understands their every need. "In the same way, the Spirit helps us in our weakness. We do not know what we ought to pray for, but the Spirit himself intercedes for us with groans that words cannot express" (Romans 8:26).

Wisdom for Daily Living

Blessed is the man who finds wisdom, the man who gains understanding,
for she is more profitable than silver and yields better returns than gold.
PROVERBS 3:13–14

*L*ord, I ask that my extended family members will know and experience Your wisdom each day. May they find that wisdom is more precious than rubies, and godly understanding better than gold. Nothing they desire on earth can compare with knowing You and following Your ways. Some of them are far from You, Lord. I pray they would learn the ways of Your wisdom, the pleasantness of Your paths, and the peace that You bring.

Unconditional Love

"If you love those who love you, what reward will you get?
Are not even the tax collectors doing that?"
MATTHEW 5:46

*L*ord, I thank You for my family members and those who are like family to me. I am grateful for their love and understanding. May I be loving in return—not only with those who love me, but even with those who are hard to be around. Your ways are merciful and kind, forgiving and good. Help me to reflect Your love, finding joy in loving others as You love me.

Living in Peace and Harmony

Rejoice with those who rejoice; mourn with those who mourn.
Live in harmony with one another. Do not be proud, but
be willing to associate with people of low position. Do not be conceited.
ROMANS 12:15–16

*L*ord, I want to be a person of peace and live in harmony with others. I know my family members, and I don't always agree. But when we disagree, help us to work through our differences and connect again with each other. Please give me empathy, allowing me to rejoice with those who rejoice and mourn with those who mourn. Make me open, Lord, to associating with people regardless of their status or position.

When I Don't Know What to Pray

In the same way, the Spirit helps us in our weakness. We do not know
what we ought to pray for, but the Spirit himself intercedes
for us with groans that words cannot express.
ROMANS 8:26

*L*ord, I don't always know what to pray for my extended family. But You know each of them—their hopes and dreams, needs and desires. I ask You to intercede with the power of Your Holy Spirit. May His deep groans translate into the words I can't express. Thank You, Lord, for filling in the gaps in my knowledge and ability. You are the God who knows all!

Don't Gossip

A gossip betrays a confidence,
but a trustworthy man keeps a secret.
PROVERBS 11:13

*L*ord, sometimes it's such a temptation to talk about other people. I like to be "in the know," but I don't want my listening and sharing to become gossip. Show me the line between relating needed information and gossiping—passing along rumors that may hurt a friend or family member. Help me to be a woman who can keep a secret and not betray a confidence. Help me to be trustworthy in all my conversations, Lord.

Healing for Envy and Jealousy

A heart at peace gives life to the body,
but envy rots the bones.
PROVERBS 14:30

*L*ord, I'm feeling envious—and I need Your help. It's hard to keep my feelings in check when I want what someone else has. Wherever I look, Lord, I see people who have something more or better than I do, and that makes me struggle inside. I have longings, Lord, but I want a heart at peace. Take away this envy and jealousy and help me to be content, knowing that You will provide for all my needs. I choose to trust You, Lord.

Accepting Each Other

Accept one another, then, just as Christ accepted you,
in order to bring praise to God.
ROMANS 15:7

*L*ord, You have made us all so different. Like a box of colored crayons, we have an assortment of opinions and beliefs in our family—and it's sometimes challenging to get along. But even though my family members differ from me, help me to respect and accept them. Help me to have a welcoming heart. Help me to love others the way You do, Lord.

Encouraging Each Other

Therefore encourage one another and build
each other up, just as in fact you are doing.
1 THESSALONIANS 5:11

*L*ord, help our family to be more encouraging. Where we've been silent, please bring kind words of praise. Where we've been angry, bring words of peace. Help me, Lord, to be a person who lifts up others by saying kind, appreciative, worthwhile things. Help me both to encourage and to receive the encouragement I need. Thank You for Your encouragement, Lord. May I be a comfort and a blessing to others.

Being a Blessing to Others

Love must be sincere. Hate what is evil; cling to what is good.
Be devoted to one another in brotherly love. Honor one another above yourselves.
ROMANS 12:9–10

*L*ord, I want to be a blessing to my extended family. I will pray for the ones You bring to mind—those who need prayer most. I bless all of them, Lord, whether I know them well or not, because You love them. Help me to be sincere in honoring them. I pray for their needs, their salvation, and their healing. I pray also that they would learn to know and enjoy You.

Praying for the Generations

O my people, hear my teaching; listen to the words of my mouth.
I will open my mouth in parables, I will utter hidden things,
things from of old—what we have heard and known, what our
fathers have told us. We will not hide them from their children; we
will tell the next generation the praiseworthy deeds of the LORD,
his power, and the wonders he has done.

PSALM 78:1–4

*L*ord, I pray for the people who will come after me—my children, grandchildren, and great-grandchildren, and even those who come after that. May they love and serve You, Lord, and make a difference for good in their generation. Open my mouth to speak of Your wonders, Your power, and Your love to my family so the next generations will know and honor You.

Praying for One Another

They all joined together constantly in prayer, along with
the women and Mary the mother of Jesus, and with his brothers.

ACTS 1:14

*L*ord, teach me to pray. And please help our family members to pray for each other. May we be focused, fervent, and faithful in coming boldly before You. Stir within each of us how best to pray for one another. Help us to develop oneness as we intercede. Give us wisdom and grace to love each other more consistently. Revive our family life for Your good purposes and Your glory.

Never Alone

*Keep your lives free from the love of money and be content
with what you have, because God has said, "Never
will I leave you; never will I forsake you."*
HEBREWS 13:5

*M*y Faithful God, I thank You that You are always
with me. I am never alone, so I don't need to be afraid.
But when I am, Lord, remind me of Your presence.
When I'm not finding the support I want from my
real family, please help me find "family" in other
people. May Your presence be near me, Lord, and
may I feel You close beside me. You are my comfort,
my strength, and my contentment.

Praying for a Family Member's Salvation

"I will heal their waywardness and love them freely,
for my anger has turned away from them."

HOSEA 14:4

*L*ord, I pray in the name and power of Jesus that You would draw my family member into Your heart. May she come to know Jesus as Savior and Lord—soon. Lord, please love this wayward child back to You. Help her to know Your amazing love, Your encouraging hope, and Your healing power. May she discover how You make all the difference in this life—and the next!

For People Who Are Like Family

Do not rebuke an older man harshly, but exhort him as if he were your father.
Treat younger men as brothers, older women as mothers, and
younger women as sisters, with absolute purity.

1 TIMOTHY 5:1–2

*L*ord, I praise and thank You for bringing into my life people I can call "family"—beyond those to whom I am related. I cherish my friends, the family of believers, and all those other people in my life who are like family to me. Keep us close and connected. Help our relationships to be loving and encouraging. Give me grace, Lord, to treat my brothers and sisters as I myself would like to be treated.

My Nation

The Power of Respect for Authority

Blessed is the nation whose God is the LORD,
the people he chose for his inheritance.

PSALM 33:12

*T*he United States of America was founded on godly principles by faithful men and women who prayed. "The Constitution of the United States, a document which has served as a foundation of the freest country in the history of the world, is largely the product of Christian men with a biblical worldview," states Dr. D. James Kennedy in *One Nation Under God.*[16]

God has blessed our country. Here, we can worship freely in the church of our choice, vote for our political leaders, and live in relative peace and freedom. But even though our spiritual heritage is rich, the moral fabric of our nation has been unraveling for decades. Many controversial social issues are hotly debated from Washington's corridors of power to the coffee shops of the Nebraska plains.

Today the need to pray for the United States—or whatever country you may live in—is urgent. As believers, we have the authority and the privilege of coming before God to ask for restoration. Revival is possible as we seek God and stand in the gap to intercede for our nation. May we never be like the people of Ezekiel's time, as described by God Himself: "I looked for a man among them who would build up the wall and stand before me in the gap on behalf of the land so I would not have to destroy it, but I found none" (Ezekiel 22:30).

We can improve the spiritual landscape of our nation with the power of prayer— because prayer moves the heart of God to action. In Exodus 34, we read how Moses successfully interceded for Israel.

How can we pray powerfully for our nation? The first step is to come before God with a heart of humility and repentance. "If my people, who are called by my name," God said, "will humble themselves and pray and seek my face and turn from their wicked ways, then will I hear from heaven and will forgive their sin and will heal their land" (2 Chronicles 7:14). With humble hearts, we can then pray for and submit to those in authority over us (Romans 13:1–7), giving them the respect and honor they deserve.

Finally, we need to remember that although we pledge allegiance to our nation, our true citizenship is in heaven. As Gregory A. Boyd writes in *The Myth of a Christian Nation*, "As people whose citizenship is in heaven before it is in any nation (Philippians 3:20), and whose kingdom identity is rooted in Jesus rather than in a political agenda, we must never forget that the only way we individually and collectively represent the kingdom of God is through loving, Christlike, sacrificial acts of service to others."[17]

God Bless America

Give thanks to the LORD, call on his name; make
known among the nations what he has done.

PSALM 105:1

I praise You, Lord, thanking You for this great nation. You have blessed America! Thank You for peace. Thank You for the freedom to speak and be heard and to vote for our leaders. We are a nation of diverse and independent people, Lord, and I pray we would respect each other. Help us to uphold godly values as we seek to honor the authority of those who govern our land. Please keep the United States united—as one strong country that seeks Your face and favor.

Respect for Authority

Consequently, he who rebels against the authority is rebelling against
what God has instituted, and those who do so will bring judgment
on themselves. For rulers hold no terror for those who do right, but
for those who do wrong. Do you want to be free from fear of the
one in authority? Then do what is right and he will commend you.

ROMANS 13:2–3

*L*ord, I pray for the men and women who hold influence and power in our nation. From police officers to Supreme Court justices, give them the conscience to do what is right—even when right and wrong seem interchangeable these days. I pray that our leaders would maintain credibility so we as American people can honor and respect them. Please help us to train our children to respect authority, as well. I pray for the integrity and morality of all who have authority in our republic, Lord.

Praying for National Leaders

I urge, then, first of all, that requests, prayers, intercession and thanksgiving be made for everyone—for kings and all those in authority, that we may live peaceful and quiet lives in all godliness and holiness.

1 TIMOTHY 2:1–2

*L*ord, I pray for our nation's leaders and ask that You would give them the ability to make wise decisions, to govern with integrity, and to accomplish their tasks in ways that build up our nation. May all the people I pray for now bring glory and honor to Your name as they serve our country: the president; the vice president; the secretaries of state, defense, homeland security, interior, treasury, agriculture, commerce, labor, transportation, energy, education, veterans affairs, health and human services, housing and urban development; the attorney general; the national security advisor; the director of national intelligence; and the Supreme Court justices.

Praying for State Leaders

Wisdom makes one wise man more powerful than ten rulers in a city.

ECCLESIASTES 7:19

*L*ord, I pray for the men and women in our state government—that they will make good policy in humility and godly wisdom. Bless their lives as they balance their work and families. Give them the strength and integrity to govern wisely. May all of the people I pray for now be faithful stewards of their office and serve the people of our state for the glory of God's name: our state representatives and senators, our governor, and our state Supreme Court justices.

Praying for Local Leaders

The prayer of a righteous man is powerful and effective.
JAMES 5:16

*L*ord, I pray that the leaders in our city and local area would lead with integrity, honesty, and fairness. May they be hungry for Your power, not for temporary control over others. May all the people I pray for now lead with justice, grace, and mercy as they serve our community for Your glory: the mayor, our judges and court officials, members of the police and fire departments, and other civic leaders.

Praying for the Armed Forces

The LORD is my strength and my shield; my heart
trusts in him, and I am helped.
PSALM 28:7

*L*ord, I thank You for all the men and women serving in our armed forces. They choose to put their lives on the line so we can have freedom and peace—and for that I am truly grateful. I ask that You would bless them for their loyalty and service. Protect them and keep them safe. Comfort them and give them strength when they are away from loved ones. Bless, too, the families who send soldiers to war or for duty overseas. I pray that You would meet their every need, Lord.

Integrity of the Family

He and all his family were devout and God-fearing;
he gave generously to those in need and prayed to God regularly.
ACTS 10:2

*L*ord, I thank You for the families in our nation that are following You and generously serving those in need. I pray that You would build more families dedicated to upholding Your values. I ask for marriages to be strong and healthy—and when they're not, please restore them to wholeness. I pray for obedient, not rebellious, children. We pray for revival across this land. May our families praise You, Lord, and put You first.

Education

Remind the people to be subject to rulers and authorities, to be obedient,
to be ready to do whatever is good, to slander no one, to be peaceable and considerate,
and to show true humility toward all men.

TITUS 3:1–2

*L*ord, we need Your presence in our schools and educational system. I pray that the teachers and administrators would lead with kindness, patience, and strength as they serve our children every day. Help them to be knowledgeable and prepared. Give them energy and good hearts. I pray for students to be obedient to the authorities in the school and to learn what they need to know. May our schools be safe places for children to prepare for work, ministry, service, and life.

Media and Entertainment Industry

"Ask and it will be given to you; seek and you will find; knock and
the door will be opened to you. For everyone who asks receives; he
who seeks finds; and to him who knocks, the door will be opened."

MATTHEW 7:7–8

*L*ord, I ask in Jesus' name that You would bring Your light to the dark places of Hollywood and the entertainment industry. Please raise up creative people with good values to write and produce entertainment that is wholesome, nourishing, and positive. I pray against the negative messages—the intense violence and sexuality portrayed on the Internet, television, and movies, and in books, music, magazines, and other media. I ask, I seek, and I knock on Your door, Lord. Open the way for a bright new day in our nation's entertainment and media choices.

Blessings for Obedience

*If you fully obey the LORD your God and carefully follow all his commands I give you
today, the LORD your God will set you high above all the nations on earth. All these
blessings will come upon you and accompany you if you obey the LORD your God: You
will be blessed in the city and blessed in the country. The fruit of your womb will be
blessed, and the crops of your land and the young of your livestock—the calves of your
herds and the lambs of your flocks. Your basket and your kneading trough will be
blessed. You will be blessed when you come in and blessed when you go out.*

DEUTERONOMY 28:1–6

*L*ord, I humbly bow before You and thank You for the
power to obey and follow Your ways. It is not easy at times,
and I know I could not do it without your help. Your Word
tells us that obedience leads to blessings. I don't want to
miss my blessings. I don't want my family or friends—or
anyone else—to miss the best in their lives either. So I ask
for forgiveness when I have done wrong and strength to
make better choices. Help all of us to walk in faithfulness,
empowered by Your Holy Spirit.

Love Your Enemies

*"But I tell you who hear me: Love your enemies, do good to those
who hate you, bless those who curse you, pray for those who mistreat you."*

LUKE 6:27–28

*L*ord, it's hard to love those people who are against me and
my country. I may not like them, but I ask for Your power to
love these enemies. Your startling and strong love conquers
fear and oppression. Help me to press through my fear,
prejudice, and indifference to bless those who hate and hurt.
I stand on Your promises, knowing that whatever may come,
our flag still stands for freedom and the cross still stands for
victory.

Healing Our Land

"If my people, who are called by my name, will humble themselves and pray and seek my face and turn from their wicked ways, then will I hear from heaven and will forgive their sin and will heal their land."
2 CHRONICLES 7:14

*L*ord, the fabric of our society has been unraveling for some time. Through our disappointments, trials, and adversities, we humbly ask that You would heal the social problems in our land. Provide for those in poverty. Heal hatred and prejudice. Intervene and destroy the strongholds of abortion, pornography, and drug abuse that ravage so many families and communities. May healing begin as those of us who believe in You call upon Your name, seek Your face, and turn from our own wicked ways—so You would hear from heaven, forgive our sins, and heal our land.

Spiritual Revival in America

*"Abraham will surely become a great and powerful nation,
and all nations on earth will be blessed through him."*

GENESIS 18:18

*R*evive us, O Lord! I pray for a great awakening of hope, healing, and salvation in America. Forgive us our personal sins and the sins of our people. May our nation fulfill her great destiny and purposes. Awaken us to our need for You and our total dependence on You. Bless us, Lord, to be a nation that is powerful—so we can be strong within and a blessing to the other nations of earth.

Citizens of Heaven

*But our citizenship is in heaven. And we eagerly
await a Savior from there, the Lord Jesus Christ.*

PHILIPPIANS 3:20

*L*ord, I am thankful to be a citizen of the United States of America. Although my residency is here, my true citizenship is in heaven. Thank You for my "passport," my salvation that allows me entrance into Your kingdom of heaven. As I journey through this life on my way to You, may I be wise, loving, and giving in my little corner of the world.

The Power of Surrender

*We become what we are
called to be by praying.*
EUGENE PETERSON

*D*o you remember daydreaming as a child about what you wanted to be when you grew up? Most of us do. Whether we thought we'd be ballerinas or baby doctors, movie stars or marine biologists, many of us have lost track of our dreams. Perhaps fear kept us from taking risks, or lack of motivation, money, or time held us back. What we wanted to become— and not necessarily just our occupational choices—got derailed.

Whatever the reasons, it's never too late to dream again and discover God's will for the next season of our lives.

Maybe you've always wanted to start your own business or go back to school. Perhaps your desire is to find pursuits that are more rewarding, such as volunteering or mentoring youth. Maybe you'd really like to have more time together as a family. Or, if you're single, perhaps you'd like to find a man with whom you are well matched, someone to share life with. Maybe it's time for a change but you just don't know how to get from where you are now to where you'd like to be.

"More things are wrought by prayer than this

world dreams of," said Alfred Lord Tennyson.[18] Praying powerfully for our goals requires us first to surrender them to God, being willing to accept God's plan no matter what the outcome. Jesus Christ surrendered with His words and His actions when He prayed with His face to the ground, "My Father, if it is possible, may this cup be taken from me. Yet not as I will, but as you will" (Matthew 26:39). God didn't answer the prayer of His own Son in the way Jesus wanted. Instead, He led Jesus to something incomprehensibly hard yet ultimately glorious. God's "no" became a bigger "yes" for the entire human race. We may not always understand God's ways, but we can take comfort in knowing that when God delays—or redirects—it is for a good reason.

As we seek God's will for our dreams and goals, we ask Him to confirm if we are headed in the right direction. Psalm 37:23 says, "If the LORD delights in a man's way, he makes his steps firm." That verse puts an image of a frozen Minnesota lake in my mind: If you take a step and the ice is solid, you keep walking. But if the ice begins to crack and break under your feet, you know it's wise to go another direction. God plants dreams in our hearts, and as we stay connected to Him in prayer, He reveals direction for every step of the way.

Prayer is the key to reaching our goals no matter what phase of the journey we're in—planning, working, or "living the dream." Prayer gives us patience, guidance, and direction. When we commit our dreams to God (Psalm 37:4–5), we can pray powerfully with sincere and surrendered hearts. We plan our work and work our plan—and trust God with the entire process.

Daring to Dream

Delight yourself in the LORD and he
will give you the desires of your heart.
PSALM 37:4

*D*ear Giver of Dreams, I believe you've placed dreams within me that are yet to be realized. Teach me to delight myself in You as I pursue the desires of my heart. Show me Your perfect will—may I move as far and as fast as you wish, never less or more. Grant me the wisdom I need to accomplish Your plans for my life and the humility to give You the glory in them.

Knowing God's Will

Do not conform any longer to the pattern of this world, but be
transformed by the renewing of your mind. Then you will be able
to test and approve what God's will is — his good, pleasing and perfect will.
ROMANS 12:2

*L*ord, I commit my aspirations to You. Give me the courage to work toward my own goals and not be swayed by the opinions of others. Renew my mind and my spirit so I will be able to test and approve what Your will is—Your good, pleasing, and perfect will. I don't have to be afraid that I will miss it—I can know that You bring people and circumstances into my life for a reason. Thank You for the assurance that You will direct me into Your good purposes.

The God Who Cares

You discern my going out and my lying down;
you are familiar with all my ways.

PSALM 139:3

*L*ord, I thank You that You are the God who cares! You want the best for me, and You are constantly designing the next steps of this journey of my life. Powerful, yet gentle and kind, You delight in giving us dreams—and the resources to achieve our goals. I pray for dreams that are worthy and wonderful. Empower me, gracious God, to be a woman of action who trusts You.

The Giver of Guidance

I will instruct you and teach you in the way you should go;
I will counsel you and watch over you.

PSALM 32:8

*L*ord, I appreciate Your wise hand of guidance. You instruct me and teach me in the way I should go; You counsel me and watch over me. What a blessing! What a privilege! No one knows my inner heart and life dreams like You, Lord. Still me and help me to listen so I can hear Your direction. And when I hear, give me the courage to walk forward knowing You are always near. You are with me every step of the way, Lord.

Trusting God's Wisdom

For the LORD gives wisdom, and from his
mouth come knowledge and understanding.
PROVERBS 2:6

*L*ord, what a blessing it is to be able to come before You—the wisest, most intelligent Being in the universe. I have direct access, straight to the top. Thank You for giving me wisdom and direction, even when I can't see the way. Knowledge and understanding come directly from Your mouth, Lord, and You delight to enlighten us. I praise You and ask for continued insight as my dreams become achievable goals.

Nothing Is Too Hard for God

"I am the LORD, the God of all mankind.
Is anything too hard for me?"
JEREMIAH 32:27

*L*ord, I want things to be different in my life—but there are so many obstacles. I need energy and motivation to get going. I need finances and more time. More than anything, I need to trust You more. Nothing is too difficult for You, Father. You can do anything! Despite all my needs and distractions, please bring into my life favor and openings—please make a way. I ask that You would help me achieve the goals in my life that are best suited for Your good purposes.

Being a Woman of Action

In the same way, faith by itself, if it
is not accompanied by action, is dead.
JAMES 2:17

*L*ord, I want to be a woman of action—a woman of true faith. Faith by itself—if only thoughts and words—is dead. It has to be accompanied by my deeds, Lord. I pray for the wisdom to know when to take risks, when to act, and when to wait. Help me to know the right thing to do and the best time to do it. Put true faith into me, Lord, so I can perform the good works You have for me to accomplish.

Trusting God's Plans for My Life

*"For I know the plans I have for you," declares the LORD, "plans
to prosper you and not to harm you, plans to give you hope and a future."*
JEREMIAH 29:11

*L*ord, You are the faithful God. I have hope for my future because of Your good promises. On You I rely. Reveal to me Your good plans for my life. As I share my dreams and visions with You, please form them into reality—or mold them like clay on a potter's wheel into something more than I ever could have asked or imagined. I put my trust in You, Lord.

God Is Faithful

The One who calls you is faithful and he will do it.
1 THESSALONIANS 5:24

*L*ord, I thank You that You are my faithful God. No one else is like You. People move away, jobs change, and much of life is uncertain. But You are always here, my stable, loving, and present Lord. Help me to hold unswervingly to the hope I profess, for You alone are faithful. You keep all Your promises—every one of them, all of the time—and I thank You for that, Lord.

Surrendering Your Dreams

Going a little farther, he fell with his face to the ground and prayed, "My Father, if it is possible, may this cup be taken from me. Yet not as I will, but as you will."

MATTHEW 26:39

*L*ord, I humbly bow before You and give You my dreams. I give up control. I surrender my will for Yours. When I am tempted to do things my way, may I seek Your guidance instead. When I am too pushy, trying to make things happen on my own, give me mercy to see that Your grace has everything covered. I don't have to be afraid, Lord. I will trust You to meet my every need.

Patience for "In the Meantime"

Be patient, then, brothers, until the Lord's coming. See how the farmer waits for the land to yield its valuable crop and how patient he is for the autumn and spring rains.

JAMES 5:7

*L*ord, it's hard to wait. There are so many things I want, and I'm inclined to charge ahead and "get it done." But You give us the "meantime" season for a reason. I ask for the patience and courage to wait well. Help me to be a woman of wisdom, knowing You have reasons for Your delays. You are not just killing time, Lord—You are ordering events and shaping my character. I yield to Your timing, Father.

God's Power to Succeed

Are you so foolish? After beginning with the Spirit,
are you now trying to attain your goal by human effort?
GALATIANS 3:3

*L*ord, I want to be Your partner in this life as we
co-labor in prayer and action. Help me to be a wise
woman, not a foolish one. I want to succeed in all
my endeavors, but I choose to surrender to You
first. And I trust that You will show me the way
to attain my goals, not by human effort, but by the
work of Your mighty and powerful hands.

Press On!

Not that I have already obtained all this, or have already been made perfect,
but I press on to take hold of that for which Christ Jesus took hold of me.
PHILIPPIANS 3:12

*L*ord, when I am weary, help me to press on. When I am discouraged, give me hope. Fill me with the power of Your Holy Spirit to persevere in the path You've put me on. I cannot live this life on my own. I know that, Lord. May Your mighty presence be in me. May Your light brighten my spirit. I ask for favor and blessing in all my tasks. And I thank You for all that You have done and are doing.

Holding on to Hope

Against all hope, Abraham in hope believed and so became the father of many
nations, just as it had been said to him, "So shall your offspring be."
ROMANS 4:18

*L*ord, please help me hold on to hope. Sustain me according to Your promises. Abraham had great faith in You, Lord, and became the father of many nations—just as You had promised him. Even though he was old, You provided a baby boy for him and his wife, Sarah. As You did for them, Lord, please fulfill my longings—and Your vision for my life's purpose.

The Power of Transformation

"Forget the former things; do not dwell on the past.
See, I am doing a new thing! Now it springs up; do you not
perceive it? I am making a way in the desert and streams in the wasteland."
ISAIAH 43:18–19

*O*n a late December day, a ten-year-old girl makes a cheery snowman with her friends. After they leave, she stays outside just a bit longer, soaking in the last moments of play and watching the afternoon fade to twilight. She listens to the wind blowing through the towering oak trees around her and to the silence that follows. In the quiet stillness, she smiles. She is happy.

As I look back on that innocent childhood memory—a piece of my personal history—I never could have imagined that day how my world would change. A few years later my parents would divorce, and I would move to another town—and then another. My spirit then could not have comprehended the devastating effect of a family member's coming illness or of breakups with boyfriends. On the other hand, I could not have expected how wonderful it would be to hold a newborn niece or to live in the majestic splendor of the Rocky Mountain foothills. On that winter day, I didn't know that the best thing to come into my life was just around the corner—and His name was Jesus.

We all have a past. We smile over some recollections.

But while many memories are happy, others hurt. We have sometimes suffered abandonment, abuse, or tragedy, and we're still harboring hurt and anger.

Though we can't change what has happened, we can change our perspective. With the power of prayer, we can learn from our past, find healing, and be thankful for the good times God gives.

The Samaritan woman we meet in John 4 had a past she wanted to hide. She had been married five times—and was living with a sixth man who was not her husband. When she met Jesus near a well at midafternoon, she was surprised that He already knew everything about her. Despite her ugly history, He offered her a beautiful future. "As far as Jesus is concerned, the woman with no future has a future; the woman with a string of failures is about to have the string broken. Jesus sees her present desire, which makes her past irrelevant," says Michael Yaconelli in *Messy Spirituality*. "Jesus can redeem our past, no matter what kind of past we bring with us: failure, mistakes, bad decisions, immaturity, and even a past which was done to us."[19]

Whether we're the ones who messed up—or whether someone else wounded us—we can give our past to God in prayer. He is able to redeem it. We can experience healing from hurt and release from pain.

It's a mystery how that transformation happens—but when we pray about our yesterdays, we can find healing for today and hope for our tomorrows.

Returning to the Lord

Rend your heart and not your garments. Return to the LORD
your God, for he is gracious and compassionate, slow to anger
and abounding in love, and he relents from sending calamity.

JOEL 2:13

*L*ord, some of the things in my past have led me far from You. I want to come back and be in right standing with You again. I ask for forgiveness for the things I have done wrong—in both my distant past and more recently. I am so glad that You are gracious and compassionate. Thank You for being slow to anger and abounding in love. Here I am, Lord. I return to You.

Forgiving Others

"Do not judge, and you will not be judged. Do not condemn,
and you will not be condemned. Forgive, and you will be forgiven."

LUKE 6:37

*L*ord, it can be so hard to forgive—especially when I feel that other people don't deserve it. But I don't deserve Your forgiveness either, and You freely forgive me when I ask. Because of Your great mercy toward me, help me to forgive the people who've hurt me in the past. Help me to know that forgiving is not condoning—but it releases me to Your freedom. I leave the retribution to You, God of justice and love.

We Need to Remember

And Joshua set up at Gilgal the twelve stones they had taken out of the Jordan.
He said to the Israelites, "In the future when your descendants ask their fathers,
'What do these stones mean?' tell them, 'Israel crossed the Jordan on dry ground.' For
the LORD your God dried up the Jordan before you until you had crossed over.
The LORD your God did to the Jordan just what he had done to the Red Sea when
he dried it up before us until we had crossed over."
JOSHUA 4:20–23

*L*ord, I want to remember the good things You have done for me in the past. Like the stones the Israelites took out of the Jordan River, I need my own personal "rocks of remembrance" of Your mercies in my life. You performed miracles for them—allowing them to cross the river on dry ground, parting the Red Sea for them—so that people today might know Your powerful hand. As I recall the ways You have helped me throughout my life, I honor You.

We Need to Forget

Not that I have already obtained all this, or have already been made perfect, but I
press on to take hold of that for which Christ Jesus took hold of me. Brothers, I do
not consider myself yet to have taken hold of it. But one thing I do: Forgetting what is
behind and straining toward what is ahead, I press on toward the goal to win the prize
for which God has called me heavenward in Christ Jesus.
PHILIPPIANS 3:12–14

*L*ord, help me forget the things in my past that I need to leave behind. Give me the courage to press on. There is a goal waiting for me, a reward in heaven—and I want to win the prize! You, Jesus, were always going about Your Father's business. Help me to face forward and move on, marching boldly into the future. I may not know what will happen from here, but I know the One who does.

Letting Go of the Past

My eyes are ever on the LORD, for only he will release my feet from the snare.
PSALM 25:15

*L*ord, it's hard to let go of things that are comfortable and familiar, even when they're not good for me anymore. I need Your strong power to release my grasp, finger by finger, on the things I cling to so tightly—like unhealthy ways of thinking or relationships that are not bearing fruit. As I release them to You, give me the courage to receive all You have waiting for my empty, trusting hands.

Learning from the Past

*Not only so, but we also rejoice in our sufferings, because we know that
suffering produces perseverance; perseverance, character; and character, hope.*

ROMANS 5:3–4

*L*ord, I thank You for Your patience as I learn important lessons from my past. I don't want to repeat my mistakes, Lord. Your ways are not our ways, but Your ways are best. They bring healing and life. As I learn to rejoice in the suffering I've experienced, I can see Your hand teaching me perseverance; from perseverance I develop character, and from character I have hope.

Living in the Present

*Come, let us bow down in worship, let us kneel before the LORD our Maker;
for he is our God and we are the people of his pasture, the flock under
his care. Today, if you hear his voice, do not harden your hearts.*

PSALM 95:6–8

*L*ord, I have been camping in the past too long. Pull up my tent stakes and help me to move on. There is so much to live for today! The past is over and the future awaits. Today I choose to worship You, my Lord and Maker. When I hear Your voice, may my heart be soft—not hardened or jaded by the past. Today is a gift; I celebrate the present with You, Lord.

Overcoming Oppression

For I am convinced that neither death nor life, neither angels nor demons,
neither the present nor the future, nor any powers, neither height
nor depth, nor anything else in all creation, will be able to separate
us from the love of God that is in Christ Jesus our Lord.
ROMANS 8:38–39

*L*ord, I ask for Your strong power to heal me from oppression. I pray against evil and for good. I pray the shed blood of Jesus over my life. Keep me safe and protected. There is nothing, no single thing, that can keep me from you—neither death nor life, neither angels nor demons, neither the present nor the future, nor any powers, neither height nor depth, nor anything else in all creation. Cover me, Lord, and be near me today.

Change Me, Lord

Yet, O LORD, you are our Father. We are the clay,
you are the potter; we are all the work of your hand.
ISAIAH 64:8

*L*ord, You know all about me—my past, my present, and my future. You are the potter and I am the clay, the work of Your hands. As You reshape my life, changing me from who I was and molding me into the woman You want me to be, help me to trust Your wisdom. I want to be a vessel sturdy enough to hold all the love You have for me—and to pour that out on others.

Truth Sets You Free

To the Jews who had believed him, Jesus said, "If you hold to my teaching, you are really my disciples. Then you will know the truth, and the truth will set you free."

JOHN 8:31–32

*L*ord, I am free! Finally! For so long I was bound in sin, selfishness, and unhealthy ways of thinking. I tried to change on my own, but like a prisoner in handcuffs, I was powerless; I could not break free on my own. Praise You, Lord—You loosed the chains that held me. Your love and strength empowered me, Lord. I choose to stay on Your path and follow the way of freedom. Your truth sets me free!

More Than Conquerors

No, in all these things we are more than conquerors through him who loved us.

ROMANS 8:37

*L*ord, my past is history. It's over and I can't change it. But no matter what has happened, things can be different from this point forward. You are the One who turns tragedy to triumph. As I look to the future, may I have hope for good things to come and victory in all I do. Let me succeed because Christ lives in me. Direct me, Lord, to Your good purposes.

All Things Work Together for Good

And we know that in all things God works for the good of those who love him, who have been called according to his purpose.

ROMANS 8:28

*L*ord, sometimes it's hard to understand why things had to happen the way they did. I have made some poor choices, but other people have done some really hurtful things to me, too. Even though I may never completely understand, I trust that You work things out for the good, for Your own glory. I love You, Lord, and I know I have been called according to Your purpose. I will put my faith in You.

God Our Deliverer

*I will praise you, O Lord my God, with all my heart; I will glorify
your name forever. For great is your love toward me; you have
delivered me from the depths of the grave.*

PSALM 86:12–13

*L*ord, I don't know where I would be without You. Your
love is so strong that You swept down to snatch me from
the gravest times of my life. You know how hard things have
been; I thought I was going to die. But I didn't. I'm still here,
and it's all because of Your power of deliverance. Praise You,
Lord! I will praise you, O Lord, with all my heart.

God Our Healer

*Even though I was once a blasphemer and a persecutor and a violent man,
I was shown mercy because I acted in ignorance and unbelief. The grace
of our Lord was poured out on me abundantly, along with the
faith and love that are in Christ Jesus.*

1 TIMOTHY 1:13–14

*L*ord, I need Your healing touch on my past. I have lived
too long in ignorance, denial, and unbelief; I thought nothing could ever change. It seemed too late. Now, Lord, please
pour out Your abundant grace on me like a waterfall. Shower
me with healing. Though I don't deserve it, heal my past
with all its problems. You have the power to cure and restore.
My healer, Lord, help me to walk in victory.

The Power of Christ-Centered Living

Instead, [your beauty] should be that of your inner self,
the unfading beauty of a gentle and quiet spirit,
which is of great worth in God's sight.

1 PETER 3:4

*W*omen love to redecorate. We watch home improvement shows, read up on the latest trends, and experiment with new paint colors. We'd never think of carefully maintaining the *outside* of our house while leaving the *inside* unfurnished.

Often, though, our inner lives resemble a neglected house. We certainly make time to care for the outside of our bodies, but many times the quality of our inner lives is lacking.

We mean well. We want to make prayer a priority, but we're chasing wandering toddlers all day. Or we'd love to sit on the sofa, reflecting on the goodness of God—but we have to get up at 5:00 a.m. for a long commute to work. The hectic pace of daily life often makes us feel more like human *doings* than human *beings.* Prayer, reflection, and rest become the empty rooms in our house of self when we don't make time for them. We need the power of the Holy Spirit to get our interior lives redecorated.

Cultivating our inner lives is not selfish—it's smart

and it's biblical. God values the inner life; the beauty of a gentle and quiet spirit is of great worth to Him (1 Peter 3:4). In Proverbs 4:23 we are admonished to guard our heart, the wellspring of life.

Taking care of ourselves, both inside and out, is vital to our survival. When our identity is solidly rooted in who we are in Christ, we have more confidence. Reconnected to the source of power and love—God Almighty—we have the resources to be cleansed, healed, and filled. And when we are rested and replenished, we have more to give away to others.

Though God isn't finished with any of us yet, we can still have powerful prayer lives when we are wellfed spiritually. Ask God for a hunger for His Word. Take time to think about what you read, and meditate on it. Pray that God would reveal to you your true worth and value in His eyes. Ask Him to help you become a woman of character and integrity, to mean what you say and to keep your promises and commitments. Pray against temptation and for the power to flee it. Don't let the evil one mess with you—ask God for help (Matthew 26:41).

Pray for the Lord to strengthen your life from the inside out, to be more positive and friendly, and to speak with truth and kindness. If you ask, He will help you find a way. In the hands of the Master, your inner life can come alive with a richness and depth that colors each part of it beautifully.

Personal Revival

May our Lord Jesus Christ himself and God our Father, who loved
us and by his grace gave us eternal encouragement and good hope,
encourage your hearts and strengthen you in every good deed and word.

2 THESSALONIANS 2:16–17

*L*ord, I have neglected time with You, and I am sorry. Please forgive me. Blow a fresh wind into the staleness of my life, and revive my spirit. Help me put aside my selfishness and seek You first. Awaken my soul to the goodness of Your love, for You are my heart's desire. Away from the clamor of television and traffic, I come into Your stillness. Thank You for causing me to linger and enjoy Your refreshment, joy, and peace.

Cleanse My Heart

If we confess our sins, he is faithful and just and will forgive
us our sins and purify us from all unrighteousness.

1 JOHN 1:9

*L*ord, I humbly ask for forgiveness of sin in my life. I repent and turn from doing wrong things. I don't know why I do the things I don't want to do. Sometimes it's willful and sometimes I'm just careless. Thank You for Your lovingkindness and mercy that cleanse my soul and let me be in right standing with You again. Cleanse me, heal me, and make me whole, Lord.

Empower My Life

"If you then, though you are evil, know how to give good gifts
to your children, how much more will your Father in heaven
give the Holy Spirit to those who ask him!"

LUKE 11:13

*H*oly Spirit, I cannot live life on my own strength. I ask that You would come and fill me with Your presence. Empower me with discernment to make better life choices and energy to thrive—not just survive. Give me a heart to seek You and serve others. Pour into my life more love, joy, peace, and patience—to be a caring mom, a loving wife, a good friend, a wise worker—a woman who is blessed, Lord.

Making Prayer a Priority

"But blessed is the man who trusts in the LORD,
whose confidence is in him."

JEREMIAH 17:7

*L*ord, I feel like a withered plant with dry, brown leaves. Help me connect with You in prayer so I can grow strong and healthy—inside and out—like a vibrant green tree. You are my source of living water. Teach me to be still, to listen, to absorb what You want to reveal to me in this time of inward filling. In this holy conversation, may I find freedom, peace, and joy—and a closer walk with You.

Living a Life of Love

"And the second is like it: 'Love your neighbor as yourself.'"
MATTHEW 22:39

*L*ord, I want to live a life of love! Show me what true love is—Your love—so I can receive it and give it away to others. Teach me to care for my neighbor as I would care for myself. Let love be my motivation for action. Help me to speak kind, encouraging words and to bless others with my actions, as well. I thank You that Your amazing, unconditional, accepting love sustains me.

Knowing Your Worth and Value

*"Are not two sparrows sold for a penny? Yet not one of them will
fall to the ground apart from the will of your Father. . . .
So don't be afraid; you are worth more than many sparrows.*
MATTHEW 10:29, 31

*L*ord, I have sought to find my significance in places other
than Your heart. Forgive me for putting weight in what other
people think or in my own efforts. I thank You that You
value me because I am Your child—and that I have great
worth no matter what I look like or do for a living. You find
the unfading beauty of a gentle and quiet spirit to be of great
worth in Your sight. Thank You for loving and valuing me,
Lord.

Beautiful Inside and Out

*But the LORD said to Samuel, "Do not consider his appearance or his height,
for I have rejected him. The LORD does not look at the things man looks at.
Man looks at the outward appearance, but the LORD looks at the heart."*
1 SAMUEL 16:7

*L*ord, our world is so focused on outward appearance—nice
clothes and good looks. But You're never like that. People
may look at the hairstyles and the outfits, but You look at
the heart. Lord, please help me to work with what You've
given me on the outside—as I also polish my inner character.
May Your beauty shine through me as I praise You more
and more. Be my light within that I may I radiate the love
of Christ.

A Woman of Wisdom

Blessed is the man who finds wisdom, the man who gains understanding,
for she is more profitable than silver and yields better returns than gold.
PROVERBS 3:13–14

*L*ord, I want to be a woman of wisdom, not foolishness. Help me to make right choices and conduct myself in a manner worthy of Your name. I pray that I would be honest and upright in my daily life so my actions reflect who You are. Help me to act with integrity, so I become a person who keeps her promises and commitments.

Confidence

The LORD will be your confidence and will
keep your foot from being snared.
PROVERBS 3:26

*L*ord, help me to have more confidence—not in myself but in You. I don't want to be proud or conceited, but I don't want to be a doormat, either. Give me a teachable heart. You have so much to show me, and I want to learn Your ways. Learning and growing, I am alive! I am totally dependent on You, Lord. Full of Your Spirit, I can stand confident and strong.

Self-Control

*Like a city whose walls are broken down
is a man who lacks self-control.*

PROVERBS 25:28

*L*ord, I need Your help. Please create in me the fruit of self-control—in all areas of my life. Empower me to walk in Your Spirit's power and to flee temptation. Help me to change the channel or walk away from the food or put my credit cards out of reach when I've been using them too much. Give me the strength I need to stay pure—both sexually and emotionally—around men to whom I am not married. Keep me, Lord, in the center of Your will.

Accountability

*Likewise, teach the older women to be reverent in the way they live, not to
be slanderers or addicted to much wine, but to teach what is good. Then they
can train the younger women to love their husbands and children, to be
self-controlled and pure, to be busy at home, to be kind, and to be
subject to their husbands, so that no one will malign the word of God.*

TITUS 2:3–5

*L*ord, I pray for someone with whom I can share my inner life—someone who will hold me accountable. Please provide a mature woman who will mentor me and keep my life struggles confidential. I pray for someone with a loving heart—a person who won't judge me but will pray for and with me. Help me to be wise and responsible, but when I'm not, Lord, help me to learn and grow in my spiritual development. I want to be strong in Your strength.

Dealing with Pride

For by the grace given me I say to every one of you: Do not think of yourself more highly than you ought, but rather think of yourself with sober judgment, in accordance with the measure of faith God has given you.
ROMANS 12:3

*L*ord, Your Word says that we are not to think of ourselves more highly than we ought, but to think of ourselves with sober judgment, in accordance with the faith You have given us. Help me not to have pride, arrogance, or conceit in my heart—but when I do, please forgive me. Humble me, Lord, and lift me up to be a willing servant. With my eyes on You, not on myself, may I see the needs in the lives of others.

Manage Time and Priorities

There is a time for everything, and a season for every activity under heaven.
ECCLESIASTES 3:1

*L*ord, help me to order my days so my priorities reflect Yours—so that I spend my time and energy as You would want me to. Amid the activity bombarding my life, center me on You. Teach me Christ-centered living so that wise choices will follow. I ask that You would give me time to get done what You want accomplished each day. Sustain me with Your motivation, inspiration, and enthusiasm for this season of my life.

A Thankful Heart

Be joyful always; pray continually; give thanks in all circumstances, for this is God's will for you in Christ Jesus.
1 THESSALONIANS 5:16–18

*L*ord, You are my God—and it is my joy to give You my inner heart. Cleanse me, fill me, heal me, and help me to live with a joyful, thankful heart. I want to be a woman of prayer. I want to make a difference in my world. For all You are and all You do, I am grateful. I give You praise for the blessings in my life.

My Future

The Power of Hope

…being confident of this,
that he who began a good work in you
will carry it on to completion until the day of Christ Jesus.

PHILIPPIANS 1:6

*J*asmine had known emotional and mental abuse for as long as she could remember. Neglected as a little girl, she grew up to jump from relationship to relationship, looking for someone to validate her worth. But it never worked—the men in her life always seemed to remind her of how horrible she felt about herself.

In time, Jasmine became suicidal. Only one thing kept her from ending her life: She couldn't think of a suitable home for her cats. After months of depression, lying on the couch and crying out to God for relief, Jasmine suddenly felt a calm inside like she'd never felt before. Without knowing why, she got up and drove to a small group meeting she'd heard about at a nearby church.

She really didn't know what she was looking for. But when the leader invited Jasmine to attend their weekly studies, she did. Though she never told anyone in the group about her desperation, the members' acceptance and encouragement changed her life. Jasmine found that she wanted to live—and she gained renewed strength and the ability to love on levels she had never thought possible. Three years later, she's walking closely with God and realizes that even though she didn't know what she was doing that first night, it led her to a future she never could have imagined.

Abram didn't know where he was going, either, when God called him to pack up his family and move to a faraway place. He was seventy-five years old. "Show me, and I'll go," is probably what most of us would have said. But Abram, in faith, accepted God's limited direction of, "Go, and I will show you." Genesis 12 reveals the whole story: Abram faced an uncertain future, but he went—and the world will never be the same.

We all have a story, and we're in the middle of it. We can look ahead either with expectant hope, paralyzing fear, or something in between. But with the perspective of God's truth, we can face the future with joy and boldness.

Prayer strengthens hope as we come to trust the One who knows all. "I know the plans I have for you," declares the LORD, "plans to prosper you and not to harm you, plans to give you hope and a future" (Jeremiah 29:11). God holds the future. Live in hope.

A Bedrock of Faith

. . .so that your faith might not rest on men's wisdom, but on God's power.

1 CORINTHIANS 2:5

*L*ord, please set me firmly on a bedrock of faith so that my decisions will rest solidly on You—not the wisdom of humans or my own fickle feelings. Strong and secure, Lord, You are my foundation. Build in me hope and faith as I put my trust in You. No matter what may happen—or what may threaten—please let my life stand firm through trials. Establish the work of Your hands, Lord, rock solid in me.

Always Have Hope

We have this hope as an anchor for the soul, firm and secure.

HEBREWS 6:19

*L*ord, please help me look forward with a positive attitude—with faith, not fear. Anchor me with hope for my soul, firm and secure. Captain the craft of my life, and keep me from wandering into doubt and insecurity over the future. I thank You, Lord, that You are in control!

Live Powerfully

Grow in the grace and knowledge of our Lord and Savior Jesus Christ.
To him be glory both now and forever!
2 PETER 3:18

*L*ord, You have all power and authority. You are the highest ruler in the land—in the entire universe! What a privilege it is to come humbly yet boldly before You and ask You to empower me today. For all I need to do, for all I need to say, may Your favor rest in me. May Your blessings, Lord, flow through my life—and may I also be a blessing to others.

Walking in Wisdom

A man's own folly ruins his life, yet
his heart rages against the LORD.
PROVERBS 19:3

*L*ord, please keep me from the foolishness of sin. I ask for wisdom and discernment to make wise choices in my life. When I'm tempted, give me the strength to flee it. When I am uncertain, help me to know the right course of action. When I need good ideas, enlighten my mind with creativity and intelligence. You know everything, Lord—may I walk in Your wisdom and learn Your ways.

A Life of Praise

Who among the gods is like you, O LORD? Who is like you—
majestic in holiness, awesome in glory, working wonders?
EXODUS 15:11

*H*oly One, I revel in Your splendor. I am amazed at all You are. Your majesty, sovereignty, and glory are a wonder to behold. That is why I praise You. There is no one like You, Lord. Let songs of worship and praise be on my tongue continually. I want to be like a lover who can't wait to tell everyone about her beloved. I love You, Lord. May I live a life of praise to You.

God Finishes What He Starts

*…being confident of this, that he who began a good work in
you will carry it on to completion until the day of Christ Jesus.*

PHILIPPIANS 1:6

*L*ord, I am so glad You finish what You start in us. You get the job done—and I'm grateful for that. You don't leave us like an unfinished project on a workbench. You don't get distracted and forget. Thank You, Lord! You have started my life, and I know You will finish the development of my character for Your good purpose in my life. Create in me integrity, faith, and joy, Lord, and help me to finish well.

The Good Life

*He has showed you, O man, what is good. And what does the LORD require of you? To
act justly and to love mercy and to walk humbly with your God.*

MICAH 6:8

*L*ord, I love to hike with You on this path of life. As we journey on, please help me to do what is good—what You want me to do. The "good life" in Your eyes is for me to act justly, to love mercy, and to walk humbly before You. Give me the courage, grace, and strength to do that, Lord. In humble adoration and grateful thanks, I look to You and walk on. I love living the good life together with You.

My Times Are in God's Hands

But I trust in you, O LORD; I say, "You are my God." My times
are in your hands; deliver me from my enemies and from those who pursue me.
PSALM 31:14–15

*L*ord, I thank You that Your hands are strong and steady. My times are in Your hands—and that's a good place for them to be. In my hands, they could fall and break. But not in Yours. Your hands create, Your hands guide and direct, and Your hands hold and comfort. I am secure in every season of my life, knowing that You will protect me and keep me safe. Hand in hand, may we face the future with hope.

God Has Good Plans for Me

"For I know the plans I have for you," declares the LORD, "plans to prosper
you and not to harm you, plans to give you hope and a future. Then
you will call upon me and come and pray to me, and I will listen to you.
You will seek me and find me when you seek me with all your heart."
JEREMIAH 29:11–13

*L*ord, I am glad to know that You have plans for me—because the future is so unclear in my mind. You desire to prosper, not to harm, me. As the giver of all good gifts, you wrap up hope and a future as my present. I call upon You, Lord, knowing that You always listen. I seek You with all my heart, Lord, and look forward with expectant hope to good things to come.

Perseverance

We rejoice in the hope of the glory of God. Not only so, but we also rejoice in our sufferings, because we know that suffering produces perseverance; perseverance, character; and character, hope.

ROMANS 5:2–4

*L*ord, I'm tired—and sometimes I want to give up. Life is not easy. In the midst of the trials, Lord, help me never to give up hope that You'll come through for me. Help me to trust Your ways and Your impeccable timing. Empower me to rejoice in hope, in Your glory, because I know everything that happens to me occurs for a reason. Through my suffering, You are producing perseverance. In my perseverance, You are building character. And in my character, You are constructing hope. Build my perseverance, Lord.

Love

"A new command I give you: Love one another. As I have loved you, so you must love one another."

JOHN 13:34

*L*over of my soul, teach me to love well. It is an art to be learned—I know I don't instinctively realize what other people need. Give me the wisdom to ask and the selflessness to give. I love You, Lord—more than anyone, more than anything. Let Your affection, care, and devotion flow through me. May I have a love-filled present and future.

Joy

*The LORD is my strength and my shield; my heart
trusts in him, and I am helped. My heart leaps for
joy and I will give thanks to him in song.*
PSALM 28:7

Lord, You are my joy. Knowing You gives me gladness and strength. As my heart's shield, You protect and keep me from harm. Help me to face the future with joy. Fill me with Your good pleasures so I may bring enjoyment to my surroundings—at home, at work, and in my ministry. Help me to laugh more and smile often as I reflect on Your goodness. In Your presence, Lord, is fullness of joy.

Peace

Do not be anxious about anything, but in everything, by prayer and petition, with thanksgiving, present your requests to God. And the peace of God, which transcends all understanding, will guard your hearts and your minds in Christ Jesus.

PHILIPPIANS 4:6–7

*L*ord, You are my peace. Amid life's uncertainties, chaos, and sorrows, I do not have to be anxious. In everything, I will pray and ask for Your help, guidance, and direction. I give You my challenges and present You my needs. I thank You for Your settling peace, which transcends all understanding. May Your serenity calm my heart and guard my mind in Christ Jesus.

We Will All Be Changed

As it is written: "No eye has seen, no ear has heard, no mind has conceived what God has prepared for those who love him."

1 CORINTHIANS 2:9

*L*ord, I am looking forward to my future with You—both here on earth and later in heaven. One day I will be changed in a moment, in the twinkling of an eye—and we will be together forever. I can't even imagine how beautiful and glorious that will be! No eye has seen, no ear has heard, no mind has conceived what You have prepared for Your children. My future is with You, Lord. You are my great reward!

The Power of Prayer

"I am the vine; you are the branches.
If a man remains in me and I in him,
he will bear much fruit; apart from me you can do nothing."

JOHN 15:5

*P*rayer is powerful. I've seen it transform lives. A prodigal I know wandered from ski towns in Vail to surf shops in Hawaii looking for life. He found only emptiness until the power of prayer brought him back to God. Today he and his wife run a Christian orphanage in the Philippines. Jim and Debbie were on the verge of divorce until caring friends, praying diligently for them, sent the couple to a marriage conference. That weekend, two broken people surrendered their lives to Christ—and now lead a growing inner-city ministry together.

The power of God makes a way where there seems to be none. Our prayers make a difference when we ourselves are connected to God. "Remain in me, and I will remain in you," Jesus said in John 15:4. "No branch can bear fruit by itself; it must remain in the vine. Neither can you bear fruit unless you remain in me." Like a branch connected to a tree, our prayers can produce an abundant harvest; apart from Him, we can do nothing (John 15:5). He is the Producer, we are the pray-ers. Our job is to stay connected.

Before Paul became the great apostle and missionary, he was called Saul of Tarsus—and he persecuted Christians.

On the road to Damascus, Saul had a profound conversion experience that dramatically changed his life (Acts 9:1–19). Soon, going by the name of Paul, he went on to preach, evangelize, and pray with vigor. He wrote of the results of living by God's Spirit—what he called *fruit*—rather than by our natural, sinful selves: "The fruit of the Spirit is love, joy, peace, patience, kindness, goodness, faithfulness, gentleness, and self-control" (Galatians 5:22–23).

Fruit is the most important indicator of the Spirit-filled life. We are drawn to women who show in their outward countenance the joy and peace flowing from within. They are not perfect, but they are forgiven. When trials come, women who are connected to God lean on His strong arms—and bounce back with resilience. They are yielding a godly harvest on their way to the ultimate harvest in heaven.

Just as a fruit tree requires sunlight, we as believers need to bask in the light of the Son, Jesus Christ, so our lives can produce a harvest of love, joy, and peace. We'll need some pruning, too, as the weight of an abundant crop requires strong branches. Be ready for God to cut away things from our lives to build stronger character and prepare us for the harvest of our prayers. "If you remain in me and my words remain in you," Jesus said, "ask whatever you wish, and it will be given you" (John 15:7). That asking is prayer.

My own life has been fruitful because of prayer. During my high school years, a friend took me to a Josh McDowell rally in Urbana, Illinois, where a woman I had never met clearly explained God's love and plan of salvation to me. I prayed with her to accept Jesus Christ as my personal Savior.

That nameless woman in Illinois never could have anticipated the fruit that would grow in my life from the seed she planted decades ago. I can't wait to meet her again in heaven and tell her about God's faithfulness in answering the prayers I have prayed.

Just as fruit trees bear a variety of crops—apples, peaches, cherries—each of us will bear different kinds of fruit, the blessings in our lives. The abundant harvest could be an encouraged friend, a stronger marriage, healthy kids, or heart at peace. For some, the harvest will be unseen fruit, a forthcoming abundance that will be gathered and enjoyed by future generations because of your faithful prayers today. In their various shapes and forms, our prayers and God's provision create a cornucopia of His blessings and grace.

Getting connected and staying connected help us to pray powerfully. Keep on praying with courage and tenacity. Never give up. Women who pray are women who love well, live victoriously, and make a difference in the world. My hope is that you will be one of them.

Let us not become weary in doing good, for at the proper time we will reap a harvest if we do not give up.

GALATIANS 6:9

Notes

[1]Max Lucado, *No Wonder They Call Him Savior* (Sisters, Ore.: Multnomah, 1986), 125.

[2]Lee Strobel, *The Case for Faith* (Grand Rapids: Zondervan, 2000), 256.

[3]Claire Cloninger, *Dear Abba* (Birmingham, Ala.: New Hope, 2005), 257.

[4]Bill Hybels, *Too Busy Not to Pray* (Downer's Grove, Ill.: InterVarsity, 1998), 15.

[5]Joyce Meyer, *Look Great, Feel Great* (New York: Warner Faith, 2006), 150.

[6]Martin Luther, quoted in *Devotional Classics, Selected Readings for Individuals and Groups*, ed. by Richard J. Foster and James Bryan Smith (New York: HarperCollins, 1993), 133.

[7]George A. Buttrick, *Prayer* (New York: Abingdon, 1942), 117-18.

[8]Kay Arthur, *When Bad Things Happen* (Colorado Springs: WaterBrook, 2002), 125.

[9]Mother Teresa, *A Simple Path* (New York: Ballantine, 1995), 7.

[10]Judith Couchman, *Designing a Woman's Life* (Sisters, Ore.: Multnomah, 1995), 136.

[11]Dutch Sheets, *Intercessory Prayer* (Ventura, Calif.: Regal, 1996), 17.

[12]Don Postema, *Space for God*, 2nd ed. (Grand Rapids: Faith Alive Christian Resources, 1997), 17.

[13]Stormie Omartian, *The Prayer That Changes Everything* (Eugene, Ore.: Harvest House, 2004), 23.

[14]Patricia Raybon, *I Told the Mountain to Move* (Wheaton: Tyndale, 2005), 24.

[15]Ken Gire, *Intimate Moments with the Savior*: Learning to Love (Grand Rapids: Zondervan, 1989), 67.

[16]*One Nation Under God*, hosted by Dr. D. James Kennedy, http://www.coralridge.org/OneNationUnderGod/constitution.htm.

[17]Gregory A. Boyd, *The Myth of a Christian Nation* (Grand Rapids: Zondervan, 2005), 93.

[18]Alfred Lord Tennyson, as quoted in *Between Heaven and Earth*, comp. and ed. Ken Gire (New York: HarperSanFrancisco, 1997), 352.

[19]Michael Yaconelli, *Messy Spirituality* (Grand Rapids: Zondervan, 2002), 60, 69.